CARIBBEAN
CRUSADE

J.F. MITCHELL

CONCEPTS
PUBLISHING

CARIBBEAN CRUSADE

A Series of Speeches

by

Rt. Hon. J. F. Mitchell

First Edition

Library of Congress Cataloging-in-Publication Data
Main entry under title: Caribbean Crusade
Mitchell, J. F. (James F.), 1931-

1. Caribbean Area—Politics and government—1945-
2. Saint Vincent and the Grenadines—Politics and government. I. Title.

F2183.M58   1989   972.950'2   89-7232

Editor: Jill Bobrow
Copy Editor: John Summers
Production & Design: Dana Jinkins
Cover: Amber Foote

ISBN 0-9611712-0-0

Concepts Publishing Inc.
P. O. Box 1066
Bridge Street Marketplace
Waitsfield, Vermont 05673 USA

DEDICATION

To my Mother

CONTENTS

Part I
CARIBBEAN UNITY AND PERSPECTIVES

Part II
STRATEGIES OF DEVELOPMENT

Part III
FOREIGN POLICY

GLOSSARY OF ABBREVIATIONS

FOREWORD

"In exploring the jungle, the explorer creates his own path, and then the path that exists is the one he has created. "

With these thoughts I ushered in my Premiership of a coalition government in 1972. The energy crisis of October 1973 made me realise more than ever how we needed to restructure our economies, plan new strategies of development, including charting a new course in constitutional progress with a united Caribbean.

The Premiers of St. Lucia, St. Kitts, Nevis and Anguilla endorsed the idea. I worked long into the night with Prime Minister Dr. Eric Williams of Trinidad and Tobago redrafting the terms of reference for an economic and constitutional analysis of the then Associated States that he subsequently financed. That and the initiative on freedom of movement with St. Vincent, St. Lucia and Grenada, agreed at Petit St. Vincent were all to flounder in the elections lost in December 1974. My interest in the theme of unity even survived a State of Emergency and hostile troops from another Caribbean territory in my constituency of the Grenadines.

These speeches have been listened to by audiences of many descriptions, from peasants and fishermen to Presidents and professors; in the streets and at banquets and conference halls. Each address led to an invitation for its sequel. The venue varied, from California to Vermont, from Vancouver to Mulungushi, from Haiti to Aruba, and at home. They cover more than two decades.

They are put together for the people of the Caribbean and I trust for the benefit also of those interested in the evolution of ideas in our part of the world.

Those who suffer the perils of winter seek a place in the sun. Yet we in the tropics, in the heat and sweat of our struggles, we long for a place in the shade. But that relaxation in the shade seems to continue to elude us!

Part I

CARIBBEAN

UNITY

AND

PERSPECTIVES

TO BE OR NOT TO BE A SINGLE NATION: THAT IS THE QUESTION

*Address to the Opening Ceremony of the
Meeting of the Authority of the Organisation
of East Caribbean States,
at Sir Rupert Briercliffe Hall in Tortola.*

May 27th, 1987

TO BE OR NOT TO BE A SINGLE NATION: THAT IS THE QUESTION

I have only touched down once in the British Virgin Islands before, and it is a pleasure to be here to get to know the place, and visit the homes of friends I have known over the years, and get a feel for the BVI.

May I first, Mr. Chief Minister, thank you and the people of the British Virgin Islands for your gracious hospitality to the Vincentians who have preceded me, and who have made their homes here. I hope they are diligent citizens, well behaved, and work hard to enhance the progress of your country. Their presence here, like other wandering souls throughout this region, creates the Caribbean family.

All these Conferences begin with persistently grand speeches on the theme of Caribbean unity, extolling the identity of our cultures and our common destiny. I have made similar speeches countless times before and am quite capable of making yet another today. But I think I'll be a little different today. Recently the tone of these speeches on unity has intensified in the region. Two of the reactions to speeches on unity that continue to haunt us are that; either the leaders are not serious and are only prepared to talk, or when it looks as though the leaders are ready to act, it is said that the leaders do not want to consult the people.

To anyone who is serious about results, it should be obvious that progress can best be made by the leaders first of all agreeing on an idea and then having the leaders getting the people to respond to ideas.

At this time in our history, I feel a strong sense of worry about the twentieth century closing and leaving us all stranded. As I travel around the world, I get even more worried. I worry when I see and study the rate of progress in the Far East, worry when I witness the impact of the battles between the Old Giants of the West and the New Giants of the East. I worry when I see the strong uniting to increase their strength, and I worry about the indecisiveness of the weak and their and our disunity.

I get a little tired of the patronising sermons on "The Role of Security in Small States", and the like. We have to behave like Grenada or Fiji to get attention, and when we stop misbehaving we are left to languish in what a constituent of mine calls "blissful obscurity".

When we, the leaders, do not discuss Caribbean unification, we are disparaged for not doing so. When we do so, we are criticised for contemplating the idea on our own. But after decades of errors, do you all really think we will repeat all the mistakes of the past!We are better leaders than that, and we intend to succeed where our predecessors failed. And if we fail again, let us see whom among us either in Government or Opposition, that history will condemn.

Many of us are ready. From my assessment, the leadership of the Organisation of East Caribbean States is ready. I have spelt out my position unequivocally in Barbados at the Convention of the Democratic Labour Party, and there I stated that I am ready to serve under any other leader. I repeat that again today. I am ready to wage a campaign in my country at any time, beginning with the present, to forge a union. But I cannot start, until both the leaders and the people of other countries are ready.

I know that when two or three begin others will follow. Some of our own people will object. Some of the critics will say we've started on the wrong foot, others at the wrong time, others on the wrong principle. But who is going to pick the right time, the right place, the right principle?

Another thing I know is that if a minimum of three countries in the Organisation of Eastern Caribbean States get started, the momentum for others will be irresistible. Over the last two decades we have seen even the most self-confident in the Caribbean among us come to an abrupt halt on their singular course, only to return like a prodigal to the Caribbean Home.

When we in St. Vincent and the Grenadines espouse the cause of Caribbean Unity and Identity, I don't want anyone to think I want an easy ride on their resources. There are none among you in the OECS who have a greater resource in tourism than we have in the Grenadines, or in agriculture than we have in St. Vincent. The fact that we are behind some of you in either is a reflection not of our resource base, but of the historical quality of our poor management in the past, and the restructuring of our economy in the last three years proclaims our capability. When we in St. Vincent and the Grenadines talk unity we are not planning to come on board or to come on stage naked.

If we in the Eastern Caribbean States unite, we will not only have an impact on the entire Caribbean Community but we will be sending tremendous signals to the small states in the rest of the world.

The Americans united 200 hundred years ago. The Germans did it and made a country out of principalities. The Italians did it. Is unity beyond us? Are you telling me that Garibaldi of Italy, and Hamilton of America (born in Nevis), could all have done centuries ago what we in the tail end of the twentieth century can't do. Can't we pull a few villages together!I refuse to believe that we can't.

Simon Bolivar created counties out of tribes and so can we.

Can't we triumph over the divisive forces in whatever shape of form they come?

When you look around the globe several countries that are powerful and significant today had their periods of disunity. The Netherlands do not have the plural name without significance. "Russia", as we know it is a union of republics. The Japanese up to 1853 suffered 700 years of local feudal warlords—the Samurai, and when Admiral Perry in 1853 forced them to provide a coaling station, because they could not defend their coasts from international powers, the Samurai decided to surrender their power to Emperor Meiji so that their country "may be able to rank equally with other nations of the world".

We are not talking about a kingdom, but in the same sense, we are talking about a single unitary state. We will not in the process become even a fifth rate power. We may begin to simply look like sensible people.

For my part I am prepared to try. I have already set out for the benefit of my colleagues my own ideas. To the public I want to say here and now how I see that we proceed.

(i) We should have a referendum before the end of this year on political union. Let us ask the people if they are interested in a united state, yes or no. Not, yes but. . . , just yes or no.

(ii) Design the Constitution.

(iii) Have another referendum to approve the Constitution after the Parliaments have endorsed it.

All must be done within two years. Let me hear those who are ready now, who will be ready tomorrow and above all let us see who will be silent.

And if we can put it together to include Anguilla, Nevis, Barbuda and the Grenadines, who will pull it apart. If the

Indonesians could keep 163 million people together on 13,000 islands what's wrong with us?

I know absolutely no reason why we should remain separated as we are. I do know thousands of reasons why we should unite, ranging from the hopeless limitations and fragility of the present system to the fulfilment of our most ambitious dream. I long to get into argument with the defenders of the status quo and the nervous ones who are scared of the act of faith that imaginative solutions demand, and this includes the groups that I call the "Yes but-ers".

Similarly too for the "Not Yet-ers". Those who elaborate the sophisticated excuse that the integration process of trade has to be deepened before it is widened. A most articulate piece of sophistry. In my view there is nothing that we are doing well by ourselves that we can't do better together. And conversely several of the difficulties like the uneven gains in the integration movement will level off as we spread both the assets and liabilities. Time will compensate.

Those of us who have the experience of Prime Ministers in these islands agonizingly recognise how frail is the confidence in our countries. Too many little things in every territory mean too much. Why many more of us don't get heart attacks and brain tumours is a mystery!And on that confidence in the country is what we depend as a people for satisfying our basic needs, and the relief of poverty.

I do admit that we can deliver more out of our existing structures and resources, as we are doing steadily to our people. But by pooling our leadership resources at the political, technical, and administrative levels we will not only see the light at the end of the tunnel, we will escape the trap of the dead-end into which we have got ourselves.

With the difficulties we face, we who are already independent, is there a future for the BVI, Anguilla, or Montserrat with independence? I do not presume to speak for the citizens of these places and while I have every sympathy for the indigenous causes of their separation, we do as Caribbean people owe it to them to provide a framework for their collective independence for they can't be colonies forever. Let me go further and say that from conversations with the British government many things are possible.

I don't believe that we have any unique problems. Our identical culture has ensured that. We suffer from the same noise pollution, environmental pollution, clock watching and all the regular prejudices.

Those who will preserve the status quo to satisfy their selfish ambitions within that status quo, or who for whatever political whim would jeopardise our progress to unity, simply categorise themselves as lacking a sense of history, of unity in the rest of the world, and also do not understand our geography. Coming as I do from a maritime background, the sea to me does not restrict sovereignty. A marine boundary expands our horizons. I go from home to government office by boat, and we can fly faster than travel by sea.

The road forward, ladies and gentlemen, will not be easy. We will have to wage war on pettiness and monumental prejudices. It will not be easy as getting Independence from the British. The British handed to us their centuries of anguish, and their wisdom in the Constitution that we now call ours. But in a sense that Constitution is not ours. It is no more than the farewell gift of a guardian. It is now our responsibility to write a Constitution for this region that embraces our own soul.

We now desperately need imaginative thinking. The goal of the leadership of the OECS on Caribbean unification must be absolutely clear. And every citizen has to stand up and be counted. Let us have the referendum on "to be or not to be a single nation; that is the question". The time is now!

FORMULA FOR EAST CARIBBEAN UNIFICATION IN THE SEVENTIES

Address at May Day Rally

at Victoria Park.

May 1st, 1970

FORMULA FOR EAST CARIBBEAN UNIFICATION IN THE SEVENTIES

During this month we celebrate the third anniversary of our party administering the Government of St. Vincent and the Grenadines. Our programme has included the building of schools and roads, the spread of health clinics, the provision of electricity in rural areas the establishment of new markets for new crops. These and similar projects have brought to you, the people of St. Vincent and the Grenadines a certain degree of satisfaction but nothing has been so significant and meaningful as our cultivation of the fertile ground of regional integration.

Today is the third anniversary of Carifta (Caribbean Free Trade Association). St. Vincent entered this association with a higher percentage of regional trade than any other territory in the Caribbean. The volume of our trade under the machinery of Carifta has grown. It is often said that the small islands are not benefiting from this trading association at the same pace as the larger. Be that as it may, I prefer to lay emphasis on the fact that Carifta has not forced a single peasant or housewife in St. Vincent and the Grenadines to purchase one single thing he or she did not freely choose. On the other hand, under the impetus of the Agricultural Marketing Protocol we have been stimulated to produce new crops at guaranteed prices which have been sold profitably to the tourist industry at home, and to marketing agencies in Antigua, Barbados, Trinidad and Guyana.

I do not for a moment wish to assert that Carifta has been an unqualified success. I am grateful to the farmers who have secured for St. Vincent such success as Carifta has to its credit in our country. The agreement is still green, and we must nurture this delicate plant with care, representing as it does a tree of life and hope planted in the Caribbean by and for the people of the Caribbean.

Apart from Carifta, we have sought and found for you, the people of St. Vincent, other ways in which we can get together with our brothers and sisters in the rest of the Caribbean to organise our common destiny. Far too often our willingness to come together becomes a reality only when we are threatened by external forces. For example, the recent unity of Jamaica and the Windwards when faced with a crisis in the banana market in Britain. Such is the fraternity of the sinking ship mentality. We will continue to go from crisis to crisis until we have permanently pooled our strength. And so we have developed other regional institutions like the Caribbean Development Bank. We have established a Central Secretariat with the most competent Secretary General we could find. We plan to coordinate further our education, health, and transport by sea and air. We have charted a course encompassing all our fears and wishes. Such a course now constitutes the mainstream of Caribbean unification today.

Still I am afraid. I am afraid that however accurately we grasp and come to grips with all that is required to consolidate the strength of the poor people of the Caribbean, our efforts will prove futile unless real gains accrue to the simplest soul in our land. Even as the agricultural marketing protocol means that he can sell two carrots at home for twenty-five cents, so must the rest of the integration programme bear fruit if he is not going to conclude cynically as he listens to the news on the result of the latest conference "All West Indian politicians do when they meet is to agree to meet again."

This brings me to the point on what has been achieved in our discussions among the small island politicians, those of us in the Associated States and Montserrat. We have formed another association, the East Caribbean Common Market. The best that has come out of this is the study the Trade Ministers and officials have done in the analysis of our separate tariffs, and our respective revenues from those tariffs. A clear picture has emerged; it is that the level of tariff on various major revenue items is similar in the Windward Islands.

It was hoped that the Common Market would stimulate industrial development in the small islands. I am now satisfied that we will not make the progress on agreement to locate different industries in different territories unless we overcome the insularity of our sovereignty. This is a point that the people must understand. The suppression of our sovereignty will provide an escape from unemployment through the development of some industrial growth. The suppression of our separate sovereignty and in its place the establishment of Sovereign unity in the Associated States, will mean more jobs and more power to the people. We must consolidate such strength as we possess if our weakness is not to increase. We are a living force and it will be unnatural for us to stay one place. Only the dead remain in a fixed position. The businessmen of the Caribbean are working together, buying and selling from and to each other. So too must the poorest people of the Caribbean unite, those of us in the Associated States.

I know we are proud of Associated Statehood. I know we are particularly proud of this constitutional status in St. Vincent, for our securing this goal has been through a tough and painful journey. I know it is difficult to part with a thing one has worked so hard to secure. We all fought in the bitter struggle for the right to govern this land. Whenever there is an electoral victory of the majority, a new sense of strength and confidence descends upon the people. It is like winning a dispute over a piece of land. I know what it is like to fight to get a piece of land. I know how difficult it is for many of you to find the money to get a piece of land to call your own. But when you have finished the battle to own a piece of land, when you have succeeded in a battle to secure the rights you long felt to be your own, your life is not finished, for on that bit of land you still have another battle to find the money to build a home for your continued security.

Even so is our position with the constitution of Associated Statehood. We have within it the title to our rights, our right to liberty, property, free speech and worship. Over us lies the protective umbrella of the United Kingdom, shielding us from the rest of the world. With Associated Statehood we are as protected as sardines. Perhaps there is much to be proud of in this state of secure preservation.

For all this security, our youthful imaginations demand more. Indeed, the United Kingdom in the Statehood constitution established the gateway to much more. To be a protected sardine is not enough. Worthy commitment toward fulfilment is the law, not preservation.

Our party in its manifesto has declared its support for Caribbean unity. Our government has stated in its last throne speech that we intend to seek association for political integration with any or all of the Associated States. That was last October. Now what progress have we made in this direction!

There have been private meetings of premiers. There have been long discussions among many politicians and private citizens. There have been many public pronouncements by certain prominent individuals which incidentally contradict their private approach to the fundamental issue. Everyone agrees that in time this unification is the answer. No problem here. But time is not on our side. We need this unification if we are to get the industries to get the jobs. The unemployed cannot forever bestow upon us their patience. Now what is the line up!

To the North, St. Kitts cannot move constructively until the Anguillan problem is settled even though I might add the Anguillans have expressed an interest in being part of a larger grouping. Antigua feels that she will evolve toward unity in time. Gently. Montserrat needs help, takes it as it comes. Dominica has not forgotten the initiative she took that induced the agony of the eight. She waits. That leaves St. Lucia, St. Vincent and Grenada.

Among us three much fruitful exchange has taken place. In all this the position of St. Vincent is crucial, in terms of our approach to the problem and because of our physical location itself. We are in the middle. We have the greatest choice. We can go with St. Lucia or with Grenada. It is not so easy for Grenada and St. Lucia without us. Indeed the three may constitute a neat geographical unit with our territorial waters smoothly defined. This question of territorial limits produces an irritation with the presence of Martinique if Dominica cared to be included.

We must address our minds to this subject and find the definitive answer. I avoid the terms Unitary State or Federation in any preliminary exposition as this only polarises opinion contrary to the genuine desire to integrate. Any framework of association must include independence and one head of state.

Carifta did not begin with the signatures of all the heads of the Commonwealth Caribbean. The nucleus was built by Antigua, Barbados and Guyana. Once the idea gained momentum, the others followed. This lesson must be pursued in the Associated States. A framework must be established by two or three adjacent territories. St. Vincent's formula of the association of "any" must be applied if ever we are to begin.

The question of capital site cannot be solved by putting names to be drawn from a hat. Our destiny cannot be molded by chance as a substitute for the expression of our will. Let us be realistic. Can we really have our children say "This is our capital that came out of a hat!" I would suggest a formula, whereby at a meeting of the three heads of the Windwards, each head be given two votes on which he must list the names of two separate places. This way each territory's second choice will pave the way to a majority vote which it must previously agree on to accept.

If only two territories meet with the object of unification then the capital issue can be solved by their appointing an arbitrator whom they choose. I am sure a West Indian scholar can be found to be trusted to do this job. Someone like the Secretary General of the Regional Secretariat could do this admirably.

Now the thorny problem of Head of State. God knows that this is the greatest problem of all and perhaps it will only be answered by prayer. At least in this we know the Church is with us. At his consecration the Bishop of the Windward Islands pleaded for Windward Island unity. We need the sincerest approach to this major hurdle. I am satisfied that this is not beyond taming by our prayers or our intellect. Whoever has the answer, let him produce it. Such a man will be the greatest here we will ever produce.

I want on this occasion to stimulate the minds of our people on this subject. Our destiny together is at stake.

Let me venture to register another suggestion. In any constitution of a Windward State, the person who is elected first Prime Minister should not be entitled to any re-election. On the other hand, the person who is elected in his place, should have an opportunity for re-election, but not for more than two consecutive terms. This way the way is open for a third or fourth person to be Prime Minister should there be a third or fourth country in the Union and so on. Now if this formula obtains, and there are two states one person could opt for being Governor General in the knowledge he can be Prime Minister for a longer time than his first colleague. Similarly if there are three states, the Premier who elects to be Ambassador to the United Nations, Minister of External Affairs and all that can enjoy real prominence while waiting in the wings without any loss of authority in his home base.

Let us not worry about Trade Ministers and such lesser mortals. There will be enough Ministries and other plums to share in any more vibrant association. Suffice it to say that the external trade of the area would be best served if coordinated by one Ministry. Similarly, finance, education, and labour will be better planned in regional integration. Little imagination is needed to know that Trade, Agriculture

23

and Tourism combined in each of three islands can be separated in three different portfolios without any pain, and in any island that is not the seat of Government, there can be a resident Minister of the territory's affairs who will live in Government House, attending the local ceremonies and occasionally drifting off to Cabinet meetings at the seat of Government.

Let us not worry about grant in aid. We can get guarantees for assistance. In practical terms there are many ingredients that must be added to any formula if we are to have a good cake. A pensions ordinance will be required for legislators so that those who have served long, with vested interests in conservative isolation, can be accommodated. If the seat of Government is in the South, then the first Prime Minister and Governor General must be from elsewhere. If the Parliament is in St. Vincent, then the Senate must be in Grenada or St. Lucia. If the Throne Speech is read in Grenada, then the Budget must be delivered in St. Lucia. Radio, television and press must assist in widening communication.

The people must visibly find evidence of their partnership. Let the Civil Service Associations work out their adaptation to a regional institution. This is not beyond the young brains among them. Indeed I am satisfied establishing wider horizons. Our Secretary General can be of enormous assistance here I'm sure.

Needless to say that in these days when we are forced to consider in depth the turn of militarist activity in Trinidad we must consider our own security in the Associated States. Independence for any single small island can spell disorder and may quickly lead to military rule.

In each island now there is a Parliament strained in legal drafting. Straining to have up-to-date laws, each parliament duplicating the other in its enactments with Ministers boasting of precedents in other territories. A lot of time will be solved by organising one brilliant legal department. We already have the machinery of a regional Supreme Court.

It is not beyond us, the people of the Windwards, or the Associated States to write a new constitution, design a new flag, write a new anthem. The question remains, do we think it is necessary?

Have we the courage to secure regional independence together? Fulfilment is the law and not preservation.

UNIFICATION:
A CONTINUING ANALYSIS

Address at Paget Farm,
Bequia

May Day 1971

UNIFICATION: A CONTINUING ANALYSIS

Unity in the Caribbean is inevitable. This unification is so inevitable that all the time not spent in accomplishing this goal will one day, if not sooner be deemed the wasted years. In turn players on the Caribbean state doing nothing toward this end, will be one day, if not sooner be deemed idlers. The inevitability in Caribbean unification renders totally absurd all the style of insular office. All the old excuses about our failure to unify are wearing thin.

Years ago when I sought your votes in this constituency, while I urged that you be convinced that I will urgently seek your best interests, I assured you that this will best be served through the unification of the Caribbean. While we in the Grenadines are being zealously watched as potential secessionists, let me assure you that out of my regional experiences as a Trade Minister during the last four years, that I am satisfied that the political leaders working toward the maintenance of their insularity, call it sovereignty if you will, are greater secessionists from the principle of unification than any old woman in Anguilla.

Being your representative has brought in its turn my position as a Minister of Government, and as Minister of Trade I have been looking after your interests at the Carifta Council. This village is typical of others its size in the Associated States in that no one can look around and find any visible benefit that Carifta has brought you. Unlike the people in other villages in the Caribbean, you can however say that you have earned some money at sea in our schooners working in the increased Carifta trade. But this does not affect more than a handful of you. Indeed such benefit as you do receive is often reduced to nothing in the abuse you suffer in certain ports of call in the Caribbean, where the goats carried on your ship are more welcome than you are. The goats do not have to pay a deposit to remain ashore and need no passport.

Still, I want to prevail on you to understand that all these islands so close to each other, need desperately to be united politically for survival. Also, if we are united we would increase our wealth, and possibly overcome the irritations we face as we move from one part of the Caribbean to another.

The only significant step made in the last year toward industrialisation in the small islands came out of the determination of the Trade Ministries in the Windwards to work together. Thus we set up in St. Lucia the factory to manufacture cardboard cartons for the banana industry and to participate in the entire packaging market in the area. The Governments of Dominica, St. Lucia, St. Vincent and Grenada, and our nationals are working in close company with Venezuelan interests in this enterprise. We succeeded simply because we were willing to suppress our individual sovereignty. Now there will be freedom of movement of goods and people in the Windwards as are related to this industry. The prototype for our industrialisation is established.

A year ago I indicated that this pattern was the only true way toward our industrialisation. Since then we have had all kinds of expensive advice. None has borne more fruit than the technique we worked out ourselves.

As I say, we continue to get expensive advice on how we may get industries in the area. One such study has been on the harmonisation of incentives throughout the Caribbean. We had hoped that this would have become the answer to the small islands' prayer, but we are not so lucky. The elaborate advice we get only reminds us that the so-called big boys in the Caribbean like Jamaica are poor by international standards and have to compete with other larger, more wealthy and at the same time still poor countries, all competing on the international scene. That leaves us in Paget Farm still fishermen, dependent on selling our catch to one another and to tourists, and hoping that the British Government will pave our streets.

The real problem is that if we are to get factories in the small islands instead of their going into a place like Trinidad, we have got to give the investor a far longer time than the Trinidadians to operate tax free in our territory. This means we will be a long time waiting on taxes to provide the cash to develop our country, to pave our streets, to help us stop begging.

You know that when the Federation became a wreck, it was said that we should have worked out a pattern of economic integration firstly. We have done this now. We even have a special grouping in the Associated States in the framework called the East Caribbean Common Market. But this grouping only identifies us as being of the same status, with the same problems, all faced with the same difficulty of being inherently small, and with the same poverty that goes with it. We just don't have the size or the resource to make an impact even on our neighbours. Among us in the East Caribbean Common Market we have little to sell to each other. A trade agreement is basically about buying and selling. A trade agreement is a good beginning. It helps you to understand your neighbours' problems. This however, is not enough.

At least we can rescue some immediate validity from the ECCM in that with the Common External Tariff we hope to create this year, we will face the world with a common front. We therefore can negotiate as a group. By this I mean no more than having a number of voices singing the same tune.

Let me at this stage extend what I have said before dealing with political unification in the Caribbean. I had outlined that the similar economies of the Windwards had indicated the practical need for their unification. Now that we are facing the problem of the threat to the banana market posed by Britain's entry into the European Economic Community, it appears patently obvious that the present economic necessity of the Windwards is basically different from those not dependent on banana exports.

But let me go further and record that while I am anxious to see our State of St. Vincent united with any of our neighbours, I am equally convinced that the integration process will only begin if any two or three islands get together, whether we are included or not. If we continue to wait for the whole region to make the leap, then we are also expecting Venus or Mars to move into the same orbit. The process has to begin with the marriage of equals. If those whose economies and population sizes are similiar do not want to get together, there will be no start at unification. It is in the context that I suggested earlier that places like the Windwards, with populations about 100,000 people, basically dependent on bananas and tourism, with therefore equal problems, sharing the same problems and therefore requiring the same solutions, should come together. In the same vein, if the near equals like Trinidad and Tobago and Guyana can't come together, who will come together with either of them? When a number of small islands combine into one sovereign state and secure their independence, then will the the way be set for a marriage of equals between the small group and a single larger independent state. Those who dream of bringing smaller chickens under their wings have certainly forgotten their own experience of colonialism.

The process of our integration in the Caribbean is like a passage through our beloved Grenadines. Beautiful as the scenery and prospect may be, there exist many attitudes that like our dangerous reefs have to be avoided at all costs. The ten minus one leaving nought philosophy, that bleakest epigram in the sensitive history of the Caribbean, still lurks beneath the smooth waters of the passage, and the atonement for its creation is still awaited. We dream of a safe passage into the shelter of a Common External Tariff. Will we be able to afford the heavy duties in the small islands, increasing our cost of living without a corresponding increase in the wealth in our own pockets? Will Carifta develop beyond merchandising or is the voyage complete!

The more I examine our problems, the more I become convinced we will not pass the reefs threatening our development unless there is a Central Ministry of Finance distributing the gains. If there can't be a Central Ministry of Finance equating the realities of anxious needs among the small islands, the job of equating gains between the larger and smaller will be even more difficult. One day the rich and poor lands of the Caribbean will have to be under the same roof, for there is none so rich here to be really wealthy should we look beyond our shores. Avoid the problems, isolate yourself as accurately as you can, we have got to take the steps one by one, resolutely and assuredly if meaningful significance is to be in our lives. All this talk of separate independence for each Associated State will not change the picture. In fact I would be bold enough to say, Independence for many of our big brothers has not saved them for the inevitability of unification. Time will only increase the urgency. The time not spent in securing this end may well be described as the "Era of the Idlers."

OUR RIGHTS OF PASSAGE

*Article Published in the
Trinidad Express.*

1975

OUR RIGHTS OF PASSAGE

Small islands, like villages, possess their own charm: a charm moulded by their nature, fashioned by time and with a style designed by their people. The village as part of a country leans on other villages for some of its needs, and thrives, in its quaintness, as part of the whole: the nation. But can the village, the island, the Caribbean mini-state keep its style, retain its identity in isolation and maintain the basic freedoms of a normal healthy society? In short, can national independence in a small island give us the good life?

Independence these days is only a telephone call away. The good life, on the other hand, such as it ever was, is receding. It was never here for many, and is getting further away even for the few. The good life to me does not mean only the belly full or a surfeit of material goods. It embraces the life of fulfilment and what I shall be dealing with in this chapter, freedom from tyranny and the very right to be alive.

The real threat to our liberty today is not from the grandiosely styled "Metropolitan presence in the Caribbean", but from tyranny within the narrow confines of the island state. For all its evils the legacy of colonialism includes certain institutions whose function is to protect the rights of the individual. As the independent authority of these institutions withers away, gradually but not so subtly, we are creating a vacuum. One day someone will fill that vacuum for us, and we will be starting all over again.

My experience as Premier, involved as I was and continue to be with with the Caribbean scene, revealed to me clearly the degree to which our institutions are threatened by the ready and unruffled acquiescence of our people. In November 1973 in my mini-state address I spelled out the problem in these words:

"Make no mistake about it, horrors of hatred, the denial of reason, the loss of a sense of beauty or the right of personal choice, and the collapse of our fundamental freedoms may well take our indifference and complacency by surprise. . . "

Caught up in the momentum of independence, the former anti-colonial politician acquires the art of control, an art that continues to be refined after independence. At some state we have got to ask the question, how do we reconcile government's quest for control with the citizen's pursuit of

33

freedom? The pursuit of independence is the pursuit of home rule. We indeed end up with rulers who are preoccupied with ruling rather than the proper administration of our affairs. It is in this context that we need to understand how our system should work, and to recognise the failures of our institutions, and so to determine the courses of action which can guarantee our freedom. For no final refuge will exist in the right language of a constitution when the insitutions upholding it have collapsed.

For good reason, every written constitution provides not only for good government, but also for good checks on government. The recent functioning of such checks on the Presidency in the American Constitution demonstrates the value in this concept. In our own anxiety for independence and the shedding of the metropolitan presence, it is even more important to avoid the establishment of a second monarchy.

This may be the place for me to record that I chaired regional meetings dealing with the Judiciary. This has given me the opportunity to secure firsthand knowledge of certain aspects of our Judicial System. Secondly I am not without experience of the structuring of the Police Service. Both these institutions relate to our liberty. To what extent these institutions are capable of securing, and continuing to secure our liberty I will now evaluate.

We can only do this by first of all recognising the value of the institutions with the capacity to be a check on government, such as Her Majesty's Loyal Opposition, the Judiciary, and the Press. Secondly we need the vigilance and determination to ensure the lively growth of these insitutions even as the country may develop under good government. In turn we need to pay careful attention to the functioning of the Police, whether they fulfil the role of maintaining law and order or if they instead merely sustain the law-makers. Experience in developing and newly independent territories has been unfortunate. All too readily the Judiciary, the Police and the Press are transformed into instruments of arbitrary rule. If these institutions function as agents of the Government and the Opposition too is destroyed, these is no check left on that arbitrary power; that is dictatorship.

THE JUDICAL SYSTEM

Justice in these islands is a very delicate plant. Indeed the image of justice in the island state is reflected in the person of a single judge. What a frightening reality that is! Imagine a country really relying on the wisdom (or lack of it) of a single intellect to sustain all the fundamental rights of its people. Not the full truth you may say, for there is the Court of Appeal, and the Privy Council. Agreed; but these are components in another dimension—time. The intervening periods between judgments can ruin faith in the system. The essential fact remains, each state has but one judge.

Judges in the Windward and Leeward Islands are appointed by the Judicial and Legal Services Commission. This body exists under the Authority of West Indies Associated States Supreme Court Order 1967. It is chaired by the Chief Justice, and includes a Justice of the Court of Appeal, a retired judge, and two members of the Public Service Commissions of the Windward and Leeward Islands holding office for three years on a rotating basis.

This system is designed to separate the Executive in the islands from the Judiciary. As such it is nobility on the quality of people attracted to its service. The first card played is already in the hands of the politicians, for it is they who fix the salaries of the judiciary. At the time of writing the salary of our judges is less than that of magistrates in Trinidad.

The regional system of appointments lends itself to a kind of impartiality that can ensure justice. It is certainly better than having a Premier or Prime Minister appointing his own Judical Commission and consequently appointing his own court, a risk that cannot be entertained. Moreover, as these islands move from Assoicate Statehood to independence, it is vital that the regional nature of the Judicial and Legal Services Commission be enshrined in the Constitution requiring not only a two thirds majority in Parliament for change, but also the added authority of a referendum. Similar care will need to be taken with providing Parliament with the right to terminate appeals to the Privy Council. In my view this should only be possible with the Intellect of Trinidad and Tobago, Barbados, Guyana and Jamaica. I must also caution that in taking this step, these small islands do so only when they can afford to meet their continuing financial responsibilities to such an institution. The Privy Council is inexpensive. We must remember that it is the poor who may need justice most.

The Judicial and Legal Services Commission also appoints Magistrates, Registrars and other legal officers in the various islands. In Antigua, Dominica and St. Kitts-Nevis-Anguilla the appointment of the Director of Public Prosecutions is made by the Governor on the advice of the Public Service Commission and in Grenada, St. Lucia and St. Vincent on the advice of the J&LSC. The Chief Justice of all these islands is appointed by the Lord Chancellor of the United Kingdom, acting on the unanimous agreement of all the Premiers and the Prime Minister of the participating territories.

Having said all this, and emphasised how the regional appointment (and dismissal of course) guarantees the most desirable level of impartiality in the Judiciary, I should draw attention to the mechanisms for frustrating the system as they exist in practice. A Premier may tell the Chief Justice that he does not want a certain person as judge or magistrate in his island. The J&LSC can be firm and make the appointment. The Premier can then refuse to provide the right kind of house, secretary or police guard. The Minister of Works can refuse to paint the house in the colour the wife chooses, or repair the leaking roof. The Governor can pointedly forget invitations to functions. Soon the J&LSC gets a medical certificate and the judge or magistrate is seeking transfer. And indeed sad judgment is sometimes made, even by a judge, such as: "He didn't get through because he couldn't get on with the politicians." This is the sort of thing I refer to when I speak of the creation of the vacuum. The lawyer may put the alternative situation euphemistically "The judge is being reached."

Impartiality in the Judicial service is being undermined in these mini-states. Impartiality on the part of the Judge or Magistrate is a matter of personal integrity, respect for their profession, and often, intellectual strength. I have already alluded to the scandalous inadequacy of the salaries in our Judiciary, and in times of economic stress such as the present, the situation is even more acute. I have also already pointed out that justice in these islands rests primarily on the shoulders of one man. A weak judge is a disaster in a small island. And as we move to independence, our solitary judge needs to know the historical role he is called upon to play. Social confidence in a small island may well collapse in the time between the first judgment and a different one in the Court of Appeal, or indeed in the length of time a judge takes to hear an injunction. It is well known that an application for habeas corpus must be treated with expedition. In larger countries the image of the Judiciary is dispersed and strengthened by the actions and decisions of various judges. The mini-state problem of the Judiciary is very much the problem of all our eggs being in one basket.

Critical as it is to witness this extraordinary importance of the single judge, we need also to evaluate the influence of the structure of the Judicial system beyond preserving our human rights. Inadequacy in this sphere does not inspire confidence in investment, and in turn, in the kind of development these islands desperately require to sustain their populations. And injustice in one island, like many other evils in our experience in this region, as soon contaminates the neighbourhood.

If our independence constitutions provide for a Barbados style amendment to the Constitution empowering our Parliament to withdraw from the regional judiciary, the mechanism for legal destruction of justice is surely at hand. Our J&LSC even as now constituted needs strengthening, for even now, in my view, it is not sufficiently strong to ensure the appropriate separation of the Judiciary from the Executive. If it is further weakened, if we ever reach the stage where each island has its own Judge and Court of Appeal, securing its talent out of the confines of a nationalism framed by 100, 000 people we could just as well forget about democracy, parliament, and the fundamental human rights.

The focus of attention therefore is on size. Justice is a quality that has to be recognised as a function of quantity. All along it is assumed that certain functions of a nation can be most efficiently administered in a small unit, a small nation. But how small do we mean, before the whole thing is ridiculous. It is a human, if you like, genetic problem. Do you, in a small society, consistently possess the range of disciplines necessary to keep a nation functioning? How finely can we define the term "nation", and apart from this consideration, let me say that the judiciary in the small independent nation suffers a great strain. The judiciary is a small closed circle. The judges do not like the burden of having to rule on one another's judgements. Sometimes a judge is promoted to the Court of Appeal and is unable to deal with a matter he has previously dealt with. He then must stand aside and leave the matter to his close colleagues. These and others like them are real human problems for our judges, and a greater problem for those citizens despairing of justice.

A further problem for the Judiciary in the Eastern Caribbean is that in functioning as a check on maladministration, its energy has to be dissipated on several governments. It is the problem of one judiciary having to deal with the different laws enacted by eight different governments including the British Virgin Islands.

For these and like reasons, the answer to the weakness of our judicial system lies in my continuing thesis: Unity in the Caribbean.

A Judiciary that serves as a check on all the islands in one larger government can surely be more effective than one having its energy dispelled on several. One Constitution, one Parliament, one set of laws can surely be more thoroughly checked and administered than several. If we really love liberty and desire its maximum expression what more do we need to justify a passion for Union of the Windward and Leeward Islands? And the problems for justice extend throughout the Eastern Caribbean, and suggest the need to embrace all the islands of the Eastern Caribbean in political union also.

THE DIRECTOR OF PUBLIC PROSECUTIONS

This is the office that initiates the judicial process. Silence here can mean murder and whitewash. It is a new office in our experience. We have been shielded historically from the power of this office for the post in colonial times was under the umbrella of a Crown Attorney appointed by the Colonial Office. With semi-independence it evolved under the aegis of an Attorney General who was a civil servant, appointed by the J&LSC With the political appointment of Attorney-General, the hope is that the Director of Public Prosecutions will be non-political. The appointment therefore of the DPP and the evaluation of his status as a prime protector of our fundamental rights need to be understood by us thoroughly.

Indeed the vigilance of the community over this office may be the only guarantee of freedom from tyranny by power-crazy ministers. Partisan affiliations should in no way be entertained in the office of DPP Yet even though the office is filled by the J&LSC the DPP may be subject to even more pressure by the island politicians than a judge.

First of all, the calibre of any person taking the job, at the salary of the DPP is lower than that of a judge. He is often a younger person, anxious for promotion. His office is structurally within the Public Service and his accomodation usually within earshot of the political Attorney General. If he does not cooperate with the Attorney General or the Prime Minister he can be deprived of typist, messenger, air conditioner and sweeper. He can be refused a loan for his car. Indeed his very appointment can be forestalled by the Head of Government saying to the Chief Justice, "You can appoint, who will pay?"

This all sounds very petty. If it does, I want to remind you that as a former Head of Government I know what goes on in the Caribbean.

Pettiness is a function of size. It is a fundamental feature of life in a small place. Pettiness can fashion policy. It cannot evolve into grandeur for such is not its nature. The growth of pettiness can only be in the geometric progression of greater pettiness. Once more our greatest enemy is our small size.

Do our people really appreciate that our Constitution in St. Vincent allows amendment by a two thirds vote in Parliament which permits a Prime Minister to appoint a Leader of the Opposition on terms approved by the Government! We can proceed in this direction until all our institutions are legally destroyed. Indeed the St. Vincent amendment to the Constitution for the purpose of appointing a Leader of the Opposition is a successful erosion of the institution of Parliamentary Democracy. For many this is no occasion for tears. Such a successful experiment is not lost on those in power. They and others emulating their example may strike again. In securing a leadership of the opposition amenable to the government's view the Government enhances its opportunities to secure the kind of Independence Constitution even more readily manipulated. The St. Vincent amendment is the abolition of integrity in the Opposition Leadership.

On this, we are well advised by the American political philosopher Madison, "There are more instances of the abridgement of the freedom of the people by gradual and silent encroachments of those in power than by violent and sudden usurpations."

Perhaps the power and status of the office of DPP can best be brought into focus if we examine some examples of the scope for justice related to, for example, a political murder. Let us take the case of the assassination of a politician, or the killing of a businessman during a political rally, or the knifing of a henchman of one party by someone in another party. If the Police say there is no evidence, and the DPP is weak or complacent the matter can be gradually forgotten and quietly buried in a verdict of "death by misadventure." If the DPP is morally and intellectually strong he can press relentlessly for justice, but if evidence incriminates the holders of political power you may one day hear that the DPP died in a car accident. Indeed if the press is relying on government advertisement to pay its editor's wages, the only commentary will be "The press release from the Prime Minister's Office."

If all else fails, the assassin's final refuge from the Police, DPP, Judge and Jury is the Committee of Mercy. His promoter may well be the Prime Minister who chairs and appoints that committee. So the Prime Minister in the ministate who has the two thirds majority to amend the constitution clothes himself with authority in the institutions he fashions about himself and can well say to the assassin "Go ahead, I will look after you."

In the light of my own experience of the Committee of Mercy I have one piece of advice which I already stated in the House of Assembly while in office. I categorically recommend that the Committee of Mercy in these islands be regionally appointed. This will hold off tyranny a little longer.

THE POLICE SERVICE

The erosion of the Judiciary as a check on Government is for the most part a subtle exercise. It is particularly dangerous for that subtlety. Perhaps the erosion won't be perceived until totalitarianism is already established. Moreover ours is not yet the community of brotherhood that will respond to James Baldwin's message to Angela Davis, "If they come for you in the morning, they'll be coming for us that night."

Because of our experience therefore, it is easier to define the method of establishing the Police State. Already the villager has experienced the police extremes—patronage and hostility.

The problem of the policeman in developing countries is

the conflict between loyalty and impartiality. The police training received at Hendon is based on the assumed moral values of British society, values such as fairplay, innocence until guilt is proven, and the right of dissent. Our societies have no similar supporting norm. Indeed ours in the Caribbean is the tradition of the folk hero Anancy, where what you are clever at getting away with is morally right. It is a primitive form of self-preservation; a self preservation that challenges the very right of others to be alive. And in the preservation of a few individuals the whole society may be destroyed.

We came through the Middle Passage from Africa to a slave society. Where are we going now? Where are our rights of passage today within our own independent country to a better life? Does Independence mean less freedom from fear than in colonial times?

So the villager knows he will be arrested if he throws stones at one political meeting and at another he will be ignored. Policemen are instructed that they must respond to calls from certain night clubs or restaurants and find excuses to abandon others. Many policemen owe their jobs to political influence, and the senior ranks thrive on promotion by a Public Service Commission appointed by the Prime Minister. The system in the islands breeds loyalty, not impartiality. It constantly deteriorates. And, I might add, British financial assistance to the police services, deliberately not documented in the budgets, does not provide us with the highly acclaimed British system of justice.

Let us for the moment imagine the Police attempting to be impartial, upholding the law rather than the Minister of Government responsible for the Police. The Minister and the whole Executive would feel they could not 'trust' the Police Force and it would become necessary, in Cuban terms to, "Arm the peasants" or the trusted aides. This situation can only instil fear or lead to civil war. Add to this the ingredient of suspicion that the Judiciary may be under political control, or amenable to it, then the least that may be said is that the country is unstable.

So the abandonment of impartiality in the Police Force, and the abandonment of fairplay among the citizens all leads to reliance on force of arms. The citizen too will have to look after himself. But in all this we shall not avoid history. Even greater authoritarianism will ensue and perhaps one day a sargeant will proclaim himself Prime Minister!

Sadly, one casualty of police repression is the intellectual. Those who are critical of the loss of freedom by the citizen are the first to be displaced for they either work with Government or in business easily responsive to government pressure. So the critics disappear, and self righteous chauvinism is enshrined. In the unstable situation capital too disappears, and with it, as in Haiti, the financial strength required to fight totalitarianism. Public apathy ensures chaos. With the collapse of the constitutional checks on the power of government, so too will disappear our fundamental rights and the very right to be alive, let alone enjoy the good life.

In our Manifesto for the 1974 election we advocated the regional structuring of the Police Force. This way we hoped to avoid many ills protecting the politician from himself and preserving the aspirations of the people. The Vincentian policemen in Antigua can be more impartial than at home. Wider opportunities for promotion would attract a better calibre of person in the Force and stabilise it as a career. This important change could be made at little cost to the various governments as there would be no problem of housing policemen on transfer among the islands. But again, will we ever get out of public apathy about Caribbean unification!

THE JURY

No review of the system of justice in the mini-state can be complete without an examination of the Jury System. Here again we are modelled on an irrelevant British system, irrelevant I may add, even for Britan itself; for the qualification for jury service is basically that of property ownership, and consequently we find a disproportionate number of shopkeepers on every jury. In developing countries, by definition, most of the society is developing, or more simply, most of the people are 'have-nots'. So the jury system is a judgment by the 'haves' on the 'have-nots', in the great majority of cases that is by the employed on the unemployed.

Moreover the small society has real disadvantages in its jury system. It is almost impossible for members of any jury to have no knowledge of a trial before they hear the evidence. They may know the person on trial, a member of his family, or friends; they may know his political connections. In like terms they may know the victim.

Very often I have compared notes on representation with politicians in larger countries. They say for example, "Isn't it wonderful for you in a small island that you can really get to know all your constituents." The answer is yes. But the disadvantages are many. And this problem of the familiarity of the jury with the participants in a trial is a serious one for the representative who tries to secure justice for his constituent.

The problem again here is one of separation of the Judicial Process from the Executive. The very criteria of selection of jurymen lend themselves to political influence. The property-owning class in the Caribbean is readily threatened. They may be very sensitive to Police protection, or desperately in need of government patronage. In many ways the Executive can spread its long tentacles and interfere with willing collaborators on the specially appointed jury list.

Yet another aspect of our 'colonial' legislation on juries needs to be questioned. It is that dealing with the Coroner's inquest. The law requires that the Coroner shall call on the Police Officer to provide "five good and lawful men" a situation hardly appropriate where the Police themselves are under suspicion as in cases of police brutality.

I stress particularly the acute problem of the judicial process in the mini-state functioning as a check on misgovernment. In the mini-state the member of the jury is easily identifiable by the politician. His station in life makes him very subject to political influence. Can we really rely, therefore, in this narrow society on the jury system to act as a check on government? If all the checks on maladministration collapse, chaos engulfs every human problem, and each ensuing day another soul is sold.

OPPOSITION AND CHANGE

Parliamentary democracy assumes progress through continuity and change. It conceives of the Opposition as an alternative government; it assumes that the checks on government function irrespective of those in office at the time. The election is the instrument of change.

But if the electoral change is pre-empted by fashioning the Commissions, the Judiciary, the Press and the Police to the Prime Minister's will, so that they each become 'handmaiden of the Lord', there is little scope for democratic change. For with the checks on misgovernment out of the way, it is a

43

tragically simple matter to gerrymander the constituency boundaries, print ballot papers to clandestine specification, rearrange procedures on the transportation of ballot boxes, allocate a suitably hostile policeman at certain polling stations. Elections there may be, but with what real choice?

So, all too easily, the principles of the democratic process may collapse. History has taught us a sad lesson here, for even a beverage as weak as mauby cannot be kept confined and bottled up too long. Power, stripped of all its frills, commissions, constitutions, and the like, is moulded in metal: the lead and steel of the machine gun. A foreign symbol no doubt, but a relatively inexpensive import for the mini-state.

EPILOGUE

I have attempted to show how the answers to the problem of justice in the small islands lie in the context of political union. The propositions are simple:

1. A Judicial and Legal Services Commission serving a single independent Union can be more effective than the same organisation serving several governments. It will attract the calibre of intellect, and provide the continuity of service in the judiciary essential to the assertion of the fundamental rights and freedoms.

2. A single Police Service Commission and Police Service for all the islands will improve the quality of the Force and reduce the opportunity for police repression.

I state these views in epilogue. I despair that they may be of only historical value, as we seem hell bent on destructive isolationism. These proposals are not that difficult to implement if there is the slightest desire for unity among the people and among the politicians. I spell them out, based on my experience, so that our citizens can see the directions in which we may go if we want our rights guaranteed in these small islands, and use their influence on the powers that be before it is too late. For the rest, I leave you to ponder two thoughts already beautifully expressed:

Lloyd Best:

"I don't know what kind of society each of you has wanted to build in the Caribbean, but I know that all of us here this evening have dreamt of something different from the order which has existed here since the days that Columbus launched the Enterprise of the Indies. "

VS Naipaul:

"Identity depends in the end on achievement, and achievement here cannot but be small. Again and again the millenium will seem about to come."

PURSUING EXCELLENCE IN THE CARIBBEAN

Address at the
Trinidad Express Individual
of the Year Award,
Trinidad Hilton

1984

PURSUING EXCELLENCE IN THE CARIBBEAN

When I was invited to speak on this lofty topic, Pursuing Excellence in the Caribbean, I wondered how I would escape a string of platitudes and maintain my controversial stature in this region. It was obviously growing to be easy to postulate the eternal truths, slip them into a Caribbean context and achieve an easy level of indifferent banality.

I want to say to the Managing Director of the *Express* that after I had accepted his invitation I had second thoughts. Mainly because I realised that today in Trinidad the most important thing in a speech one makes is not what is said but what is left out. And in a speech to congratulate a medical doctor, who am I to offer any medicine to Trinidad?

I wish to congratulate the *Express* on what I consider to be an important attempt to establish our heroes. Nationhood is meaningless without targets of excellence, and when, in our context, performance has been achieved, we must find a way to acknowledge it.

Dr. Courtenay Bartholomew has made his mark on the medical profession here. He has produced results that are not only recognised here, but appreciated in the wider international community. To bring medical expertise from all over the world into Trinidad annually not only broadens our horizons but it ensures that in the competitive international jungle our existence is recognised. I am sure you would wish to express your appreciation for the annual medical update, and it would be appropriate if the update not only pays attention to the sensational (in more ways than one) subject of Aids, but continues to examine our own problems of high blood pressure and sugar.

I am personally pleased to congratulate Dr. Bartholomew for his work on the restoration on the Catholic Cathedral. As we begin to learn the importance of architectural design and begin also to learn to respect our environment, it becomes even more important to preserve our heritage particularly when those old buildings built a century ago are more elegant than the matchboxes we put together today.

Sometime ago while I was in Opposition a British architect came to see me and said that he was planning a design for a new Parliament building for St. Vincent and the Grenadines as part of the Independence grant. I told him that if I formed the government and he designed anything less gracious than the old existing edifice, that I would return the parliamentary proceedings to its traditional home.

The project did not get off the ground. It became obvious that the standards to be imposed on us through technical assistance were far inferior to what the Colonial masters conceived for themselves in the days of their own glory. It is for us, the leaders in the various sectors of life in the Caribbean, to be the ones to limit our own ambitions.

More recently I refused to open an ugly building in Kingstown that spoiled the appearance of our city. Another aid project of my predecessors.

While we can set our standards in architecture that enhance our environment, I am afraid we are falling down on more basic principles. As I travel around the region I wonder who among us will win the title of the Garbage Capital of the Caribbean. Our people do not seem to understand that the beauty of our landscape is the responsibility of each and every one of us, and not that well known scapegoat, the government. It is the responsibility of sanitation authorities to move refuse from collection points, but our country will never be tidy if our citizens are not repulsed by their own littering habits.

I spent three formative years of my life in Trinidad as a student at the Imperial College of Tropical Agriculture. I regret that I have to say that Trinidad then was cleaner than it is now. Perhaps increasing pollution is proof of your progress. But do not think I am castigating you. I am not pleased with the littering in my own towns and villages.

It is very difficult for me to lecture in Trinidad and Tobago without recalling my experiences here. I have planted thousands of cocoa trees both in Trinidad and Tobago.

Some twenty-four of us West Indians were in the class at the Imperial College. Seventeen fell by the wayside. If you failed a single subject you were thrown out. In those days English and Foreign students exceeded our West Indian members. There was no joking then about achievement. We were being trained with great sensitivity to be the bosses of the natural resources of the tropics. When I hear today about strikes on the campus by students over trivia unconnected with their studies I think it is time we return to the standards of the past, and send them home when they fail a subject. We cannot afford to waste our expensive time at the University. I have recently visited the Pacific and learned about productivity in that part of the world. We have a long way to go if we intend to sustain the kind of standard of living for which we now have appetites. If we bowed to one another as they do in South Korea we would swear that slavery has returned to our culture. The South Koreans are graciously bowing with a 7% growth rate all the way to the bank. The rate at which they are going in the Far East they will in due course dominate the world's banking system.

When we get certain signals, like the statistic that the average Japanese student at 17 years of age knows more mathematics than his American counterpart, what does it means to us in reference to our educational standards. What kind of goals do we have, and how do we propose to get there! The fact that we are doing better than some developing countries, such as sub-Saharan Africa, is no excuse for complacency. The speed at which serious countries are going means that we must continue to move at an ever increasing pace if only to remain where we are.

When we meet on an occasion such as this, commending a University Professor of Medicine for his own work, what also matters is that the message goes forward that our society becomes success story motivated. We must not allow the syndrome "all ah we is one" to inhibit our love for excellence. That "who she playing" type of criticism in the Caribbean has got to stop, undermining our achievers, imposing on them a sense of guilt about their performance. As I said earlier, we have to establish our heroes. We have got to be proud of success. The safety of the haven of mediocrity is a foolish illusion.

But the "all ah we is one" syndrome has even more disastrous results. It takes on a new dimension when it embraces the revolutionary fervour that surrounded the word 'Equality' during the French revolution, and when it means for the rebels in our culture that the best should be broken, be it in business or calypso composition. Equality cannot mean that we must all aim to be equal in the gutter, equal at the bottom of the ladder of achievement. Equality for us means that we aim to become a Willie Demas or a Sir Arthur Lewis. It does not mean that we abandon our roots. Metaphorically we must also have some beautiful flowers.

Nor will I say that excellence in our own environment is good enough. The breed of chauvinism that specifies that our standards must be our own and must in no way measure up to international criteria is not my cup of tea. And this is where the question of our identity as West Indians arises. Your own V. S. Naipaul said it eloquently and simply

"Identity depends on achievement." We need to repeat this over and over. And all those Caribbean people who are culturally lost will get the answer they are looking for when they address themselves to the implications of that statement.

For all those struggling with the quest for our identity as a Caribbean people let me remind them about Christopher Columbus. He was the first genuine West Indian. He set out for he knew not where and when he got there he didn't know where he was.

The next area of my concern is our sense of history. What we accomplish must not only improve our circumstances or conditions around us, it must stand the test of time. Is it really enough that the melody of calypso be good enough only for a season? Except for political satire in some countries, written or cartoon, there is no part of the world where there is a better social commentary in song than in the Caribbean. But my concern is about the musical ingredient. How many of our songs are identifiable when you hear the band playing and there is no voice? How many of our tunes will inspire another generation at another time?

Leonard Bernstein, the composer of the great musical "West Side Story", was recently my guest at home in Bequia. To listen to him really enjoying himself playing Chopin's Waltz Op. No. 2, on piano, like the virtuoso that he is, was a fantastic spiritual experience. All of us who heard him could neither believe our ears nor our luck. We told him so. "But", he replied, "what would I have given to have composed it!"

Another regular visitor to Bequia is Professor Kuhn, a Mathematician from Princeton. He told me how Sir Arthur Lewis instructed his attendant, on the day the Nobel Prize for development economics was announced, to say he was not there.

I learned a lot from those responses. If when others tell you that you have reached the top and you yourself believe it then you are a lost soul.

Only Jesus Christ had that luxury to define for Himself that His job on earth was done. But even He went one step further when He commended His Spirit. It should always be our aspiration to let the things we have done and the principles for which we stand inspire others.

LANGUISHING IN PEACE

*Address at the Opening Ceremony of
the Sixth Conference of
Heads of Government of the Caribbean,
Barbados*

July 1st, 1985

LANGUISHING IN PEACE

I wish to thank the Government and people of Barbados for the excellent arrangements made for the hosting of this Conference.

Let me congratulate you, Mr. Chairman, Honourable Bernard St. John, for assuming your role as Prime Minister of Barbados. Let me also put on record my appreciation for the co-operation and the areas of assistance my Government has already received from you, Mr. Chairman.

I remember well in 1957, Mr. Chairman, when we met in Barbados to chart the course of Carifta, the Caribbean Free Trade Association. I was then a Trade Minister. We embarked on an exercise that consumed our time, far into the night, in Georgetown and many other Caribbean cities. Indeed, to get Carifta into Caricom, for many a session, we worked far into the night. For me it was a real pleasure to sign the Caricom Treaty, for we were in those days enthused with the expectation of the early seventies. Some who toiled in that vineyard have perished, and I am still hoping that those early efforts were not in vain.

Mr. Chairman, I was then, in those early days, of the view that there was still hope for possible joint political independence for the smaller islands of the Caribbean, and staked my political fortune on that premise.

After the Community Treaty was established, I moved into opposition in my own country. When the Constitution of St. Vincent was amended to make the wife of a Minister in the same political party as her husband, Leader of the Opposition, and this constitutional misdemeanour was greeted in silence by the leadership of the Caribbean, I began to wonder if the Caribbean Community for which I had given so much even had a conscience. Nevertheless, I have returned.

Mr. Chairman, we are all very jealous in our definition of sovereignty when it suits our selfish purpose. I remember watching a television programme on Grenada, here in Barbados, in the company of other Prime Ministers, on the protests taking place in Grenada, before the independence of that country. We were shocked, but we said nothing publicly. I still wonder if the course of history might not have been different if the decisions on freedom of movement which Grenada, Saint Lucia and St. Vincent had taken at Petit St. Vincent had been allowed to mature and grow. All that was not to be.

Now that we are nearly all for the most part sovereign and independent, I would hope that we could face the rest of the world with an opinion that deserves respect. My Government stands firmly on certain international issues, in that, like the international community, we do not condone apartheid in any form, but we do certainly think that the voice of the Caribbean condemning apartheid would carry more weight if democracy in this region is not in any way curtailed, and if we uphold the principle of free and fair elections. We should take the beam out of our own eyes, before we seek to dessicate the moat in others.

I know that support for human rights may still only be at the stage of platitudes in the Caribbean, but that does not deter me from indicating my view that we need a Caribbean Commission on Human Rights.

We welcome to our fold, Mr. Chairman, the Representative of the duly elected Government of Grenada. I hope we are all wiser for what is described as the Grenada experience. But in the aftermath of that experience, while Grenada reverts to what may be described as normalcy, I detect a certain external indifference to the Caribbean because of that normalcy. The economic and social problems that created the Grenada Revolution have not vanished from the Caribbean, even as the rate of job creation does not match the rate of population growth. I detect the resolution of that revolutionary experience to be hanging like a veil over us.

The veil of comfort is the antithesis of conflict. The image of the Grenada veil conjured up in the rest of the world is that, now Grenada is settled, the rest of the Caribbean can be left to languish in peace.

But, whatever perception we may have of the way the international community views the Caribbean, or whatever perception we have of the international community, our best defence, our best strategy, is to put our own house in order.

This is the best way to prepare for the economic hurricanes still to come.

Mr. Chairman, we of the OECS territories are still less developed territories and I would hope that when all is said and done, it is understood that this region will not be successful if steps are taken regionally that undermine development in those territories without the scale of operations to withstand certain pressures. Likewise, whatever we can do to strengthen the economies of our more fortunate neighbours, we will do so, for in the spirit in which Lincoln guided America many years ago, we will not get profit in the Caribbean by weakening the strong.

There are serious difficulties in trade in this region. And I do hope we will be able to resolve some of the issues at this meeting. There are great numbers of our people unemployed who will be listening to the proceedings of this meeting to know if there is any hope.

There can, of course, be no serious growth of trade in the region without a corresponding growth in the economy of member States. We have to guard against blaming the Caribbean Community for the resolution of some our internal problems in our member states. Blaming the institutions which we are supposed to control, while providing a scapegoat it does not provide the answer. Within this framework, Mr. Chairman, I must also address my concerns over the recent developments in the regional airline—LIAT. While we are on the one hand telling the international Community that we desperately need aid on concessional terms for our development, and mobilising our forces to fight IDA graduation, it is to me more than passing strange that we should in this regard, be turning our backs on concessional financing as we are doing with financing LIAT. We should, above all, be sending consistent signals to the international community.

Then there is the long unresolved question of British West Indian Airlines based in Trinidad and Tobago, that seems to be forever unsettled. I remember the question being with us since 1967—BWIA, to be or not to be, the regional question! Since 1967, now for 15 years, we seem pathologically incapable of answering for BWIA that Shakespearean question—to be or not be the regional airline.

One other issue that will be foremost in the minds of the St. Vincent and the Grenadines delegation will be the problems of citizens face as we go through the international airports in this region. This kind of problem sounds like a trifle but, if solved, it will tell our people a great deal about the meaning of the Caribbean Community. We ask not for freedom of movement, only ease of passage.

Mr. Chairman, these Heads of Government Meetings always end with signing Declarations. We have had the Georgetown Accord, the Chaguaramas Declaration, and the Nassau Understanding.

I hope that at least we will end up this meeting with nothing less than a Barbados Understatement.

CONCLUDING THE CENTURY WITH CONFIDENCE

*Address at the Barbados Democratic
Labour Party Conference.*

August 1st, 1986

CONCLUDING THE CENTURY
WITH CONFIDENCE

I wish to thank you most sincerely for inviting me to address your Convention. I pray that my contribution will merit the honour you have bestowed on me in this period of renewed glory of your Democratic Labour Party.

Let me again congratulate your Party on the extraordinary success you attained in the recent general elections. Fortune does not always exceed our political expectations, so let me warn you early that the pendulum does not enjoy being swung to extremes; it prefers to swing about a norm. I must thank you for winning the election, since I had lost one hundred dollars to one of our political colleagues in the region in the St. Peter by-election and I was therefore pleased to have him return the money on the general election.

It has been very fascinating for those of us who keenly study the political direction of our region to see the way events recently unfolded in Barbados. Time and time again a country seems to like to torture itself, experiment with fantasy and illusion only to create opportunity for pure and genuine leadership. Many people in and out of Barbados, and indeed many out of this party and indeed in this party did doubt the leadership of the Democratic Labour Party only to return to the realisation that the vintage material of your Leader, Errol Barrow, could not be bettered.

Let me tell you here and now, quite a lot of people outside Barbados have not yet got the measure of Errol Barrow, your tried and tested old soldier. Those who have this difficulty really don't have time for some of us in the leadership of the Caribbean because we don't fit snugly into the pre-ordained cubby holes they have designed for us. Some of our own people are annoyed because they don't know which way we are coming from. Their real problems are that they do not take time to assess our philosophy of life, or to realise that we know whence we came and where we want our people to go. The simple truth of the matter is that the most difficult person to deal with is one who is not greedy.

Nothing now more clearly demonstrates the empathy that exists between Barbados and St. Vincent and the Grenadines, and the psychic experience we share, than in our seeking a guest speaker at our respective conventions. One morning I called your Prime Minister to invite him to be our guest speaker at the New Democratic Party convention in Bequia, which is to be a joint function with the 20th anniversary celebration of my parliamentary life. Errol chuckled. So I had to repeat that the invitation was serious. Then he said, 'But Son, I was just about to call you because my Executive last night took the decision to invite you to be our guest speaker on the same day!' We could not believe the coincidence. So I had to persuade my Executive to change our day, so that I could be with you today and have your political leader with us next Sunday.

Your Prime Minister and I are old friends. My old friend Philip Greaves who had earlier left me in Hampstead and returned to Barbados, introduced us when I too was returning home through Barbados on a banana boat. Let me reveal to you a story of my recent history. You will recall I became notorious on the West Indian political scene when I negotiated my way into becoming Premier of St. Vincent in 1972 when two major political parties tied with six seats and I was cast in the centre as an Independent. There are two men to whom I owe a tribute for the outcome of that resolution. One was Robert Lightbourne, the famous Jamaican Minister of Trade, who taught me all I know about negotiation, and the other Errol Barrow, who sent through a message that was not to be quoted "Stand firm, you can do it"!

I think that the present level of political cooperation between us, having other political leaders in the region at our conventions enhances the process of our governmental cooperation. Indeed, strengthening the bonds between our political parties is fundamental toward any eventual political unification.

Last year we hosted Prime Minister Charles at our New Democratic Party Convention and I spoke at the 21st Anniversary Convention in St. Kitts. Cooperation at this level laid the framework for the Mustique meeting which tried to bring Guyana back into the Caribbean mainstream.

While every Caribbean Government will have to work with any other Caribbean Government in their common interest, it is so much easier when you are dealing with a kindred soul.

Before you think, Mr. Chairman, that I am here setting up a love affair between St. Vincent and the Grenadines and Barbados, let me hasten to get a few things off my chest that have been smouldering for a long time.

Barbados really offended a lot of us in December 1979, when Barbados troops took over the Grenadines. I want to ask you a question: Is there a single Barbadian who relishes the thought of Vincentian policemen coming up here to keep you in line?

When the Government of St. Vincent was crazily seeking help to control half a dozen young men in Union Island, I had a call from the US Embassy asking me what I thought about the situation. I said that I was sure that nothing could happen in Union Island that I could not handle in a swim suit. The young people of Union Island were simply vomiting in revulsion at the thought of another five years of Labour Party abuse of the Grenadines. In due process, we became a tool in the justification of military expenditure in Barbados.

While I was the first person to publicly declare when the murder mystery was being staged in Grenada that we owed it to the silent people of Grenada to seek help on their behalf, I think the political leadership of this region must distinguish between fighting the enemies of the people and our own legitimate dissent under incompetent mismanagemant.

Barbados troops in pursuit of rebels in Union Island even tore up the floor on one of my old family buildings, to find nothing. The reason why I did not sue for damages and trespass is that I myself and thousands of Vincentians have to trespass at Grantley Adams International airport on our way home and we have to constantly lean on your hospitality.

When the State of Emergency abated, I called on your former Prime Minister to use the moral authority of his participation to press the St. Vincent Government for a Commission of Enquiry into the Union Island disturbance; he replied that it was an internal matter.

The night of our general election in 1984, your coastguard was in our waters with Vincentian policemen waiting to arrest me. They were there in anticipation of yet another uprising that was to follow my defeat. The gods determined otherwise.

With these experiences, perhaps you can understand why I find the subject of regional security so boring.

I was only too happy to show forgiveness when I invited your former Prime Minister to the same Union Island when we were helping the creation of the New National Party in Grenada. Our hosts in Union Island for lunch that day and who provided us with a house for the meeting were none other than the distinguished Adams family who too were incarcerated during the State of Emergency for their cardinal sin of supporting the New Democratic Party.

All this is behind us. You people of Barbados are on a new course. In my antimilitarism I was isolated, but with the DLP victory I am no longer alone. We all know that we want our peace to be protected, we want our happiness to be ensured. We are not blind to our security needs especially the threats of corruption that haunt us with the drug trade. Your Prime Minister and myself have agreed to maintain cooperation on security but we will not place any emphasis on militarism.

But no military might in the Caribbean will protect us from the ignorance in our midst, the self-righteous strains on our resources stemming from teenage pregnancy, and the rising expectation of our television culture. And the truth of the matter is that we in the Eastern Caribbean who have been managing our economies moderately well need little wind in our sails to reach the promised land.

The future of the Caribbean depends on the economic strength of each of our territories individually and collectively. Let me put you in the picture about what we have been trying to do in St. Vincent and the Grenadines.

When my New Democratic Party took over the administration we found a situation where there was:

(a) the government account in deficit;
(b) the statutory bodies and government companies were operating without budgets and writing cheques as they pleased;
(c) accountablilty had gone out of the window;
(d) we had twice the national debt we assumed at election time; and
(e) the National Bank, our main financial instution, was overdrawn.

We had to begin fulfilling our election pledges to reduce taxation, and we had to begin our structural adjustment from day one.

Early in the life of my administration, I had a country meeting with the World Bank and IMF in Washington and outlined what my strategy was going to be. I did not know then that they were cynically saying to themselves "we have heard all this before from every new administration the world over". By last year June, when I made my presentation to those august bodies and the international donor community, they could only say "congratulations are in order".

We are meeting all of our financial obligations both inside and outside the region and I am being forced into embarrassment with my colleagues in the region who resent being asked 'why can't you do it if St. Vincent can?' God knows our economy is vulnerable and dependent on others. We are lucky that our people are industrious and that our leadership has decided to keep on course. My politics emerges from the experience of the sea. I know that no matter how turbulent the voyage, as long as the Captain can bring the ship to a safe anchorage, the crew and passengers will eventually say thanks.

We had to close down the sugar industry, a project conceived like bringing back the old time religion and without reference to common sense, let alone economics. You who have relied on the industry uninterrupted for three hundred years may not know how to pull brakes even though you are running in a race that the more astute have abandoned. We lost $42 million in five years and consumed most of our workers savings in the process with nothing to show for it.

Fortunately, we have not been dependent on sugar as you are in Barbados. But you the people of Barbados, whom I once described as constituting the haven of commonsense in the Caribbean, should not find it beyond your ability to overcome the challenges with which the chemistry of sugar has burdened you. Out of my knowledge as an agronomist of the soil and environmental conditions of Barbados, your choice of an alternative to sugarcane will not be easy, but it will be a problem you will not be able to avoid addressing, and I wish you the best of luck.

Barbados has been singularly successful in maximising the usage of its resources up to the present time. As to whether or not you will face the next century with an economic basis of confidence will depend on the decisions you take about the sugar industry, and whether or not your people in the tourist industry keep pace with mechanisms which will guarantee the quality of life to which your educated masses will aspire.

I was delighted to hear that you are about to embrace the Singapore model of industrial development. In conceptualising this, your leadership is trying to bring you in tune with the realities of the excessive competiveness of

65

today's world. I really wonder if our people can continue to look backward to slavery as a justification of the level of productivity known as laziness. Or will we have to go through the downward spiral of poor productivity, over value our poor performance, and create the necessity for devaluation; so that instead of attaining a regular pace of accomplishment, we return to the bottom of the ladder to start climbing again.

If we think we will unobstrusively drift toward the twenty-first century without courageously adjusting to the realities of the marketplace, and simply keep praying that the conscience of the industrialised world will put something our way, even as we pander to the lowest common denominator in our own society, seeking always the elusive goal of ephemeral popularity, we will simply miss out on opportunity to create a new order without even knowing it.

As we look to industrialisation as a means of curing our unemployment problems we have got to look at our external competition and examine the level of productivity elsewhere. What I have seen in South Korea and Japan tells me that we have got a long way to go. Moreover, their level of service serves notice that many of our workers in the Caribbean workplace should be arrested for loitering.

No money spent in sending people from the Caribbean to experience what is going on in the Far East will be wasted. Let me give you some examples:

I witnessed a ten-minute break period in a car factory in Japan. When the break period was sounded, no worker on the production line who was fitting a part stopped working until his part was installed. In our situation the worker would be anticipating the break and would not be caught with something in his hand. Electricity was cut off for nine minutes to save cost in the ten-minute break period.

Japan is thirteen hours in time ahead of New York. Japanese executives, financiers, and foreign office personnel go to work from nine in the morning and work up to 11:00 p.m. at night so that they not only start their day thirteen hours ahead of New York but are working at night when the New York day begins. Young foreign service personnel are prepared to put in seventy-eight hours a week from Monday to Saturday and volunteer for work on Sundays, and put up with three days holiday a year during their probationary period. These are the people we are trying to catch up with. The truth is that every day we are falling more behind.

We in the Caribbean are far behind in development. How far are we prepared to refine our work attitudes to give us the life styles and consumption patterns we say we want.

Another experience that stunned me in Japan was to see workers doing keep-fit exercises right on the job. They are prepared to exercise and tone up their bodies during working hours to increase their productivity. The Minister of Fisheries told me that he took part in public exercises with 10,000 people.

Personally, I am quite prepared to honour trade union demands for forty-hour and thirty-five hour working weeks, but for myself my country would be poorly served if I confined myself to those hours and did not put in an extra two or three hours a night.

I have made reference to the industrial pattern of work in the Far East as it affects our opportunity to produce for the international marketplace at competitive prices. The same goes for our tourism product. The people running and serving our airlines should also be exposed to the standards in the Far East. Out there, they really know what it is to sell a service.

Sir Arthur Lewis in a Caribbean Development Bank presidential address once made the point and it bears repeating. He said that when you go into a store in the West Indies you you are greeted "What do you want?" When you go to buy something in the developed world the attendant politely says "What can I do for you, Sir?" What a difference! The sooner we realise that we can assert our dignity and get for ourselves the income and quality of life through excellent service, the more pleasant our lives will be and our contries more enjoyable. The battle is not lost for many of us have learned the lesson; but I am afraid that we are a long way off as a people, whether as politician, businessman, or worker from establishing for ourselves a tradition of brilliant service. Those who do are successful. Those who don't fall by the wayside and they wonder why. Some of our fools enjoying the status of certain office believe that by rudely keeping people waiting they are asserting that we are now independent countries and that they are showing off their national sovereignity. All those attitudes in my view are guaranteed to impact on our slow rate of development, and guarantee no more than our sovereign poverty.

Looking at Barbados from the perspective of our problems at home, you in Barbados have two things going for you. One is that you have, and have had a good educational system for a long time, and you have your population growth rate under control. Your people have already perceived the importance of control of numbers, but by and large our people in the other islands have a long way to go in this regard. If we continue the way we are going in St. Vincent and the Grenadines, early in the next century our numbers of people will exceed yours. I don't know what kind of neighbour we will be if that happens. Heavens forbid! Your level of education and the common-sense of the ordinary Barbadian shows itself all the time. But I'm going to tell you a story that really brought this home to me.

In 1974, when Joshua resigned as Finance Minister from our coalition government and said that he did so because there was no money in the Treasury, a seaman on a Vincentian ship told me of his experience on reaching Barbados shortly after. As the ship came into the Carenage in Bridgetown, he threw the line ashore for a man to pick up. The Barbadian said to him. "Man, what kind of people you Vincentians are. You got a Finance Minister leaving the Treasury and boasting that he's broke. Jump ashore and hold your own line, you hear!"

Barbados has been educating the Caribbean a long time. I have myself passed through the hands of several noted teachers to whom I must pay tribute. W. M. Lopey, who served St. Vincent for thirty years is the greatest headmaster St. Vincent has ever had. He has made an indelible mark on thousands of us. He did of course have a great idiosyncrasy as a classical scholar; when you chose to go into the Sciences rather than Latin, he made you feel as though you were abandoning the opportunity to be civilised. Then U. G. Crick hammered into me the most of what I know in mathematics and paved the way for me to deal with the IMF and World Bank. He left me with a piece of mathematical philosophy that has guided me in much of my political career. "Mitchell", he used to say, "a straight line will always cut a curve."

The question that now remains with us, in the light of our long and close association, is how do we enhance the relations between our two countries to make the association more meaningful. How are we in the light of our personal understanding of each other to bring the relationship into greater maturity.

First of all, there are a few arrangements we have to get out of the way. God was not kind to St. Vincent in giving us any flat land as you have in Barbados and as a result you have an international airport and we don't. You know how important is the opinion of Barbadian nationals in London and New York on political life here. The same thing goes among our expatriates. Whenever I have to speak to them whether in High Wycombe or Montreal, the one question I have to answer is, when are we as Vincentians going to have an easy time passing through Barbados. Why do we have to go through Customs and Immigration when in transit through Barbados?

Why when we are returning to New York through Barbados do we have to go through immigration and customs when all we want to do is go through security checks and get on the international flight? Your Government has agreed to examine the problem along with the airlines and we hope to have the matter resolved to our mutual satisfaction. If we can't resolve these simple problems then the more difficult issues will be long in being solved.

I want to make a suggestion for cultural exchange between our parties. I would like to invite you to consider a programme for members of our parties hosting the children of one another on short vacations. This will be a great way for our party supporters to create linkages between the islands. The arrangements I am sure can be made through our respective secretariats.

So much for my concerns in our bilateral relations between Barbados and St. Vincent and the Grenadines.

But where are we heading in this region as we face the twenty-first century? Will we be concluding this century with confidence? Will we have come of age as a nation as the twenty-first century dawns, with a Caribbean confident of its role in the councils of the world or will we be still groping on the world's stage waiting on others to sustain us.

I claim neither the gift of prophecy not infinite wisdom but there are several questions that out of my experience I would like to leave with you.

The first relates to the broad question of political unity, for no matter how skilfully we develop our own islands, that question will not go away.

Will the 21st Century find us still divided with each leader confining his energies within our liquid borders, playing the role circumstances prescribe, with some seeking escape trying to be a more sophisticated auctioneer of national sovereignty than his neighbour?

Whenever discussions on any form of political union arise, public opinion loves to blame leadership and declare that the foremost reason for lack of progress is the selfishness of leaders who want to be king fish in a small pond rather than rock hind in the wide ocean. Let me speak for myself and place on record that I am prepared to work in any Cabinet led by certain other colleagues in the leadership of this region now. I know some now in opposition too that I am prepared to work with. Both Errol Barrow and Eugenia Charles could win an election in St. Vincent and the Grenadines, with my help of course. Tom Adams would not have done so, not after sending troops into Union Island. But he would have won in Grenada, of course!

My only reservation is that I cannot go to bed with the communists. Life for that is too short. I won't be able to sit quietly and watch anyone mismanage our resources, ignoring the history of the world or our own geography.

The public and the press have got to determine a way to push the leadership toward unification bearing in mind that cream will always float to the top and that it is the dregs that will be discarded.

The next thing is this. Will there be a single constitutional structure that will work or should we go for unity with diversity (if such a monster makes sense). The fashionable accommodation that was building up before October 1983 and vanished with a single geographical push, and the swing of public opinion back to the Caribbean norm should tell us that there is a norm for this region and that the political extremes are only a waste of time. If even nothing happens in my lifetime I want to place on record my point of view. I don't think the Westminster style of government will keep us united. Cabinet style horse trading for Constituency benefit won't work. The guiding force of a President needing votes in every village will in the long run create the greatest harmony. We should not only look at Presidential models but particularly at the French and the leadership of De Gaulle creating a new constitution in an old and mature European civilization. Then too, we should study the West German constitution as a model, which creates strong party mechanisms, strong constituency representation, and strong provincial government, yet with the unity essential to sustain a foreign policy that of necessity has to be strong and coherent.

Even Britain will have to go through Constitutional evolution if that country is going to respond to the economic pressures from the Pacific in the next century; so we should not let the 21st Century catch us with the anachronisms of Westminister.

On the economic plane, will we begin the next century with vibrant economic growth fulfilling our needs or will we be like our brothers and sisters in much of Africa and be worse off than at independence? Will we be cursing our environment for its inadequacies when we are the ones ruining the environment.

Will our friends in Trinidad be able to live with oil at $16.00 a barrel and recover their economic leadership? They used to do quite well at $3.00 a barrel. Quite frankly, will the next century find our leaders closer or will they be even more than ever hiding from one another like children in a playroom?

Will Guyana still be in debt, with the weeds, insects and organisms that are agents of decay being more in control of the county than the military forces? Will their border dispute with Venezuela still be not settled while restaurants flourish in Caracas and you can't get a loaf of bread in Georgetown? Will the people of Guyana assert the leadership which the skilful use of their resources should dictate?

Will any of us really be ready for the industrial restructuring that the world desperately needs to overcome the debt problem? I have already alluded to the quality of your education in Barbados, but are you really ready to fine tune your intellect to what is really required for industrial or tourism success? Are you ready to take up your arms, your hands this time to fight against people pursuing industrial excellence like a crusade.

I get so mad when I hear people talking about working like a slave. We have established a name for ourselves internationally as good cricketers. It's about time we get known for something else. What's wrong about being known as the most industrious people in the world. We like our hang ups about slavery and have no strategy to overcome that experience. Look at the response of the Japanese to Hiroshima. They are seeking economic power with a vengeance. Look at the Jews. Nobody is going to get another Jew into a gas chamber. They don't even need the United Nations for their survival.

Our failure to determine our goal and establish a strategy of accomplishment will remain our enemy. To me there are only three forms of power; the power of the intellect, the power of the gun, and the power of money. The masses should be another category, but the weight of the masses depends on the force of the intellect that leads or the guns that suppress. Look at the comparative strength of Israel and the Arab world and you see what I am talking about. I may sound cynical, but those who want to talk black power better get hold of one of the instruments I define. If I have to choose which I consider most important I would go for the power of the intellect, education, technology and all in this particular sphere. With this orientation the rest will follow. The point is made philosophically in the Bible "In the beginning was the word. "

I cannot close without expressing social concerns about our environment.

Will the 21st Century find us a drug-free zone? I think this is more important than being the zone of peace that those who love military control are always talking about. To tell you the truth, when somebody passes me with a large transistor radio ruining the peaceful scenery or when I want to go to sleep and noisy so-called music is ruining the serenity of the Caribbean I wonder if I can't get those instruments back where they came from and get a real zone of peace. Those things worry me more than nuclear fission.

Will our architecture ever match the beauty of these islands that God has given us?

Will we ever get excited about the real opportunities through imaginative agricultural restructuring or will our dreams of salvation only come the noises of the new religions booming from the street corners? We will not make it to Heaven if our agricultural production policies keep us genuflecting before deaf priests at foreign altars, while presistent frustration creates new crimes.

Will we escape the cycles of boom and bust? It is only natural that when you are doing well, like Trinidad in the oil boom, you feel confident, you don't feel you need anybody. Come recession, you need friends, you need markets, you get a Nassau Understanding*. All this is simply a reaction to external forces. It is not a result of conceptualisation from within.

And so as we go from one question to another in crisis

72

management.

Do we really have to devalue two hundred percent to come to our senses? Even that doesn't seem to work if we evaluate our Caribbean experiences. People don't seem attuned to economic reality. They prefer calling for the new Messiahs who have traditionally led us into the wilderness. Sometimes they go the other way, do nothing and say they prefer the devil they know, and they call it playing safe. They did that in St. Vincent in 1979 and ended up with $45 million debt in the sugar industry.

Will we ever produce a Brahms or a Beethoven adding a single tune to the melody of this world? Will one percent of our people in twenty years be able to converse in the language of our neighbours in Latin America? Will we have the Caribbean known as a sensible place? Will we continue to trap ourselves in the smallness of our economies? What are our strategies for the new dimensions?

*The agreement made by the Caribbean Governments in Nassau to increase tariffs on goods coming from outside the Caribbean.

THOUGHTS ON THE
EAST CARIBBEAN UNION

*Discussion Paper presented to Heads of
Government of the East Caribbean, St. Lucia*

October 13th, 1986

THOUGHTS ON AN EAST CARIBBEAN UNION

During the 1986 Annual Meetings of the Boards of Governors of the International Monetary Fund and the World Bank, there were several country discussions in which the Prime Ministers from the Organisation of East Caribbean States participated. After one such breakfast session on September 29, held to discuss the development of a regional vocational and technical education project, I invited my colleague Prime Ministers Herbert Blaize and John Compton to address the subject of political unification and to make a categorical declaration indicating where they stood on the matter.

We all agreed that we were positively committed. The Prime Minister of Grenada suggested that we discuss the issue further in St. Lucia where we were scheduled to meet again on 13 October 1986.

What follows is the paper which I presented on that occasion in St. Lucia to Prime Ministers Herbert Blaize, Eugenia Charles, John Compton and Kennedy Simmonds along with Vaughn Lewis, Director General of the OECS Secretariat and Gus Compton of the Secretariat who was our host that evening. Lester Bird was invited but could not attend.

The proposals set out in the paper were agreed to in principle, and it was agreed that a technical committee be appointed to address the various issues attendant on their timely implementation.

On Saturday, 15 November 1986, I held a briefing session with the Committee which comprised Willie Demas, Alister McIntyre, Vaughn Lewis and Crispin Sorhaindo.

Following the OECS meeting in Antigua on 29 November, all the Prime Ministers met with Lester Bird and informed him of the decisions taken in St. Lucia, and of the appointment of the technical committee.

The basic text of the document, (with minor changes) presented to the OECS Prime Ministers, follows:

THE LESSONS OF OUR INDEPENDENCE

1. Whatever status we enjoy as Prime Ministers at home, the moment we have to deal with the International Community and reply to the question: "How many people do you represent?" — we experience deflation. The perspective

of our smallness and lack of importance on the world stage comes home, whether we are talking to someone from Europe, Asia, Africa, North or Latin America.

Economic realities now are clearly telling us that we will not mobilise the resources to fulfil our people's demands on a continuing basis as we are now structured. Whatever we do, we could do better if we were one legal entity.

2. Many financial institutions find it impractical to offer loans below a fixed floor level—usually around US $25 million. None of us can singly handle a loan of this magnitude for any infrastructure project in one year. We will be able to prepare, fund, and execute several such projects if we were one legal unit. We will also generate the technical competence to do so on a continuing basis if united. If we have civil servants assigned to certain specialised fields, we will develop a broad scope of expertise.

3. The economic realities of the future are even more bleak. Each of us is still largely mono-culturally oriented; sugar, bananas, cocoa, tourism. Within the framework, we will simply be unable to make the structural adjustment to our economies required to enable us to recover from natural or economic shocks over an extended period. In the face of unfavourable external realities, we will continue to stagnate relative to our population growth at home, and the rate of progress in the rest of the world.

4. Our linkage to, and dependence on, European protection for bananas will not be a route to genuine independence. Even if our bananas remain protected into the next century, tying our independence to the vagaries of British politics and the value of the pound, is perilous policy. In any event, our negotiation of protection will be enhanced by unity.

5. A single legal unit will deliver more goods to our people.

6. Freedom of movement of people, finance, goods and services will stimulate growth and inspire new confidence.

7. Security will be enhanced in a single archipelagic state

with wider boundaries. We will be more important to the security of the United States, Canada and Latin America if we have a single voice speaking for a large strategic area. This will improve our negotiating position in seeking to access funds for development.

8. Our Civil Service and Police will have better career opportunities. The Union will attract professionals home, and curb the brain drain from each of our territories.

9. The security of our country with one coastguard and police structure will be enhanced.

10. With our graduation from concessionary financing from the World Bank our individual needs for the financing of capital projects from external sources will inevitably lead to an increase in our debt burden. Sharing the administrative and other fixed costs of borrowing would help to alleviate this problem.

11. Our present limited ability to benefit from economies of scale is likely to worsen and reduce the feasibility of development projects. Coming together is the only way out of this dilemma.

12. Financial union will attract finances.

CARIBBEAN DEMOCRAT UNION

We are all, except Antigua and Barbuda now members of the Caribbean Democrat Union (CDU) with the same political philosophy. The time for us to unite is therefore fortuitous. If we do not come together now, it will not happen again. Other political parties in the region, of other complexions, will also need to unite.

WHAT WE NEED TO DO!

1. Define immediately a broad and mutually acceptable constitutional framework for unity and cooperation.

2. Having determined the framework, decide on:
   (a) A strategy for implementation; and

(b) A feasible time-frame.

(c) Decide on the level of local government to be retained.

AREAS TO BE AVOIDED

Charting any course for the present and future must draw on the experience of past failures.

1. Words like 'Federation' must be avoided at all costs.

2. The squabble over leadership must also be avoided. I am sure a framework can be devised to create an enhanced political future for every leader, and create roles of meaningful international significance.

3. Squabbles over "capital site" must be solved by anticipating them with imaginative thinking. There is no reason why the administrative centre should be in the same island as the Parliament. There is no reason why administration should not be centralised in some cases, and decentralised in others so that each island has a sense of real function and leadership.

THOUGHTS ON A CONSTITUTIONAL FRAMEWORK

1. A single Republic with a President elected for a single fixed five-year term.

2. The President, as in Latin American Constitutions, should not be capable of succeeding himself, and must be succeeded by someone from another island. Any president may have a second term, but not successively.

3. The President should be elected on the French Constitutional model, with more than 50% of the votes. If not there must be a run-off between the two front runners.

4. The President shall appoint a Governor in each island to be his personal representative during his period of office. The Governor will in turn be supported by political deputies of Ministerial rank.

5. There shall be an elected Parliament on the West German model—50% of the votes based on proportional representation (party votes) and 50% on a constituency basis.

Political leaders through the proportional representation system will have their continuity ensured, more so than under our existing constitutional framework. The area will be better off for it by using our experience, both those in Government and Opposition.

6. The size of the Parliament will have to be assessed. The structure of the Parliament could be rationalised as follows:

(1) For five States, fifty seats.

(2) Assuming an island population of 100,000 people, seats on proportional representation and five on Constituency representation (or it could be six and four. (Alternatively, the proportional representation seats could be allocated in the traditional manner, with the whole new country treated as one constituency, and a minimum threshold of say 5% of votes cast to earn a seat.)

(3) The number of proportional representation and constituency seats will need to be rationalised on the basis of population.

(4) There will need to be a minimum threshold for, say, Anguilla. Each island unit in this category should have a distinguishable seat; Anguilla, Barbuda, the St. Vincent Grenadines, Carriacou, and Petit Martinique. Nevis, of course could be embraced in a suitable structure.

7. The Parliament or Congress will be legislative. The President should be free to choose his Cabinet from inside or outside the Parliament. Any leader who therefore campaigns for the Presidency and is not in the Parliament will be entitled to a role in government.

8. The President should have the right to dissolve parliament and call an election for the remainder of the parliamentary term.

9. The election of President and Parliament should be simultaneous.

10. The Parliament should be able to impeach the President with two-thirds majority, provided the decision is upheld in the Courts.

11. The President should not be able to dissolve Parliament if impeachment proceedings are initiated.

ABOLITION OF POST OF GOVERNOR-GENERAL

Needless to say, in this process of constitutional reforms the post of Governor-General will be abolished.

We should retain the Queen in her role as Head of the Commonwealth.

PRIVY COUNCIL

We should not try to force too many changes on our people at once. Serious consideration should be given to retaining the jurisdiction of the Judicial Committee of the Privy Council, leaving changes in this and other pertinent areas for subsequent consideration.

INTEGRATION OF LAWS

Special attention will need to be given to the consolidation and unification of our laws—ensuring the applicability of one body of law throughout the legal entity devised. Obviously, transitional arrangements will have to be put into effect.

The experts will have to determine the validity of our separate constitutions and law to establish a new Supreme Law.

A great deal of funding will be available for this and quite promptly. With computers and word processors the job will be simplified. The First Congress or Parliament will have to a lot of work to do. Existing rights and obligations will have to be protected and enshrined.

LEVEL OF LOCAL GOVERNMENT

No constitutional structure of unity will get off the ground unless there is early determination of the role of local government to be retained out of the existing structure. Unless, however, there is a firm commitment to vest in the Central Government powers of taxation and revenue collection in respect of customs duties, consumption taxes and income taxes, the proposals are doomed. Nor will the Union be capable of negotiating serious development loans.

The responsibility of the local government must be defined early. There has to be the political will to settle it. Technical draftsmen must have clear guidelines.

OVERSEAS REPRESENTATION

We spend about 4% of our Budget in St. Vincent and the Grenadines in contributions to overseas institutions. This is the price of independence. On top of all this, we spend more on our Embassies abroad.

Should we be a single unit, all these costs (which are constantly escalating) will be reduced to one payment.

None of us as self-respecting Prime Ministers will take the job of being Ambassador for the OECS as now structured. The record of payments is too disastrous. But I am confident that as a Union, several positions will open up in overseas representation—United States, OAS United Nations, Canada, London, Brussels, Latin America, the Far East. We can ensure that there is a rationalisation of members among our various citizens in the postings.

Such an Ambassador will have more clout. He can be a past President, or future President, or Minister.

Moreover, there will be savings on all the meeting expenses that Ministers and Civil Servants attend, without diminishing meaningful representation at conferences.

EFFECT OF AUTOMATIC CUSTOMS UNION

From the moment we establish a legal union, there will be automatic movement of our citizens, finance, goods and services. Competition will reduce prices, markets will expand. Business confidence will be enhanced. Service industries will take on new dimensions. Gone will be the work permits, alien licences etc. among us. There will be new dynamism in the Region. We will not have any fears of dominating one another. Our homing instincts will remain, but will be stimulated by new freedom in the escape

from insularity.
THE CENTRAL BANK AND CURRENCY

If all the OECS territories combine in one unit there will be better coordination of policy on finance, including currency. If any remain outside the new dispensation, then special arrangements will have to be made for them.

OECS TREATY

The treaty will have served its purpose and be defunct.

INTERNATIONAL SUPPORT

I am confident that we will marshal a great deal of international support for a new Country. We already have experience of the so-called independence grants from the United Kingdom and the slow disbursements of the Canadians. We will be able to negotiate sensible proposals now and maximise our our foreign policy credentials. The United States, United Kingdom, France, Canada, Venezuela and Colombia will, I am sure, make meaningful contributions. International and various multilateral institutions will respond positively.

NAMING

A new union will pre-empt our colleagues in the region and we will arrogate to ourselves the right to be called Caribbean people. What else can we call ourselves but the East Caribbean.

THE ALTERNATIVE

The alternative to our scenario of union is the status quo. In that status quo, we the leaders will soon fade out or go under, one by one. We may even vanish with boredom from the scene. And the same fate, in due process of time, awaits our successors facing the escalating problems.

I think we can all work out a system we want for ourselves. I cannot believe it is beyond us. We are like-minded people who trust one another.

We will be failing our children if we do not, with our joint experience, chart the new course. The decision is entirely ours. We can fashion the institutions to our liking. We do not have to re-invent the wheel. We know the ridiculous weakness of the Westminster system and how it slows down development. We can learn from models elsewhere, and people with the knowledge of those models will be only too anxious to help us.

We have to take a bold leap forward. We have the ability, the imagination and the experience to define the path. Gradualism will not be enough.

DECISION

To summarise, we need to decide:
(1) The principle of Union.
(2) The level of local government.
(3) The strategy of implementation.
(4) The methods of implementation:
(5) Date of simultaneous referendum on new constitution in every island.
(6) Date of first election.

My own opinion is that the referendum should be no later than end of 1987 and election by Easter 1988. Those who are ready should proceed immediately. St. Vincent and the Grenadines will be prepared to go with a minimum of two other states. We would prefer, however, to be with all the OECS territories, and Montserrat and Anguilla. To entertain the BVI at this stage may also slow down progress. We know what we have in the cohesion of the OECS, the fraternity and the shared experience. We will be expanding our horizons.

We have to avoid the emotive words of failure like "federation". The theme would be better marketed as; 'Reuniting the Caribbean.'

TIME TO REFLECT: TIME TO EVALUATE

*Address at the Miami Conference
on the Caribbean.*

November 19th, 1986

TIME TO REFLECT: TIME TO EVALUATE

Mr. Chairman, distinguished delegates, ladies and gentlemen: I think it fitting that with the Caribbean Basin Initiative a few years old that we ought to pause and re-assess what gains we have had from what was heralded as a great window of opportunity for our countries that constitute the Caribbean Basin.

I deliberately did not come to this centre stage in Miami before as I thought it best that I should wait and see how my own country benefitted. Now that I have not seen very much benefit I thought I should come to the Miami conference and see what's going on for myself. For in classical Biblical terms, when you are doubtful about what can come out of Nazareth, the injunction is that you should come and see.

I had some earlier reservations and many of those reservations still hold good. The security concerns in the Caribbean region were conceived by the US as a foreign threat, while we on our part saw the root cause as the social and economic conditions on which the foreign influences play. Those social and economic conditions have hardly changed, and there is still need to promote the right conditions for trade and investment both in the Caribbean and the United States.

I emphasize the right conditions both in the Caribbean and the United States. For while we are prepared to accept all the lectures about our investment climate, if protectionism renders our Caribbean efforts null and void, then we are getting nowhere. It takes two parties to make a successful wedding ceremony, no matter how willing the priest may be.

Mr. Chairman, we have always welcomed the centrepiece of the CBI, namely, preferential duty-free access of a wide range of products imported by the US from the region. But there are a number of factors which explain why we have not grasped the opportunity.

First and foremost, our infrastructure has to be in place. It would be naive to think that we could seriously motivate our private sector or that of the US to exploit these fantastic new opportunities if we do not have a proper road network, good transportation facilities including airports and seaports. Reliable power generation and telecommunication systems have to be also in place.

Of course, one is cognizant of the less than adequate Economic Support Program (ESP) of some $350 million which was part of the Caribbean Basin Initiative, but this has long been exhausted. Indeed, any serious program of aid for the Caribbean which aims in the long run at bringing about growth and development, must be accompanied by adequate financing to take care of our infrastructural needs.

Not only does poor infrastructure inhibit the local private sector, but it also serves as a disincentive to the foreign investor who initially may have an interest in a particular country.

A case in point is my own country. Two weeks ago a group of investors from North America came to St. Vincent and expressed a keen interest in investing in a plant to manufacture certain types of supplies. Naturally, one of their questions was whether we have a good water supply system. In all fairness I had to acknowledge that the kinds of supply figures which they had in mind would be far more than we could ever provide at this point and time. I used this as an illustration to demonstrate what I am talking about when I say that the infrastructure must be in place if we are to realise tangible benefits from the Caribbean Basin Initiative.

Needless to say, in our part of the world and given the economic malaise which plagues most of our countries there is keen competition among ourselves to attract foreign investment. I have no doubt that these investors to which I alluded earlier will make their way to another island where they perceive that the water supply conditions might be adequate. For myself I am not in the business of engaging in "cut-throat" competition. Investors must do their homework and determine the territories in which they wish to invest based on their findings. My country will welcome any serious investor in both the industrial and tourism sectors.

We in the Caribbean will continue our efforts to attract new investment, but I want at this juncture to welcome USAID's offer to support the establishment of an Eastern Caribbean Investment Promotion Office. We know we need training in the market-place, even as your investors need to know our countries. There is a lot of snow in Montana but simply giving us a pair of skis will not make us enjoy skiing. We'll break our legs, and similarly, the American will break his legs if we give him a coconut tree and tell him to to help himself to some coconuts.

To my mind, more jobs, more investment, greater productivity, and more trade are the only solutions to the present social problems which threaten each and every Caribbean territory. On top of all the problems of education, over-population, and centuries of neglect we have a new monster to deal with, a monster invented in the US, and that is the problem of the drug scene.

If we are going to talk about industrialisation, economic stability and productivity in the small islands of the Caribbean, we must address the constraints. I think it is already well known that drug trafficking absolutely ruins agriculture. The drug plants suffer from no disease or pest, and are far easier to grow than winter vegetables. I want to make one point in passing, we need to direct some of the funds now allocated to drug prevention in the United States to research in biological control of these plants. It will really help if we can infect marijuana and the coca plant with some diseases.

The other economic level to which we must pay attention at this Conference is the impact of the drug traffic on industrialisation. It is far easier to make money in the drug traffic than slog away in a factory for a sweltering eight hour day.

And finally in this area of concern, let me state that the drug Mafia with their vast resources can easily destabilize a poor government, and if the United States does not work sympathetically with us in providing alternatives to the drug trade, the longed for industrial miracle in the Caribbean will be relegated to the millennium.

The majority of us share the same vision of the democratic ideals as the people of the United States. Caribbean opinion was with you on Grenada even though the rest of the world cried foul. You moved with us to remove the Communist menace, and we are both beneficiaries. But the balance is weighted in your favour, as you have more to lose from communism than we do.

I do hope that we will not suffer the same fate in our cooperation with the United States in drug control.

Again, I want to acknowledge in passing the very recent discussions which were held between USAID and our Industrial Development specialists and the commitment on the part of AID to strengthen through technical assistance and financing those agencies at the national levels charged with the responsibility of industrial development. We in the region applaud such an initiative and trust that those resources so allocated would be sufficient to bring about real benefit to our countries.

While we acknowledge these initiatives on the part of the United States we consider those goods which are still not included under the CBI to be a serious limitation to fostering greater trade between the English-speaking Caribbean and the United States. I refer specifically to apparel and leather goods which are excluded from duty-free access into the United States market.

It is true to say that the provisions under Article 807 go some way toward redressing the total exclusion of garments for duty-free access under the CBI arrangements, but one must always be cognizant of the limited manufacturing capability of island states like my own. This is because we lack the technology that would foster a deepening of the industrialisation process. Unfortunately, the limited technology issue was not part and parcel of the Caribbean Basin Initiative. I am, of course, very pleased with the new Presidential awards for training and in this regard I am delighted with the new avenues that may be opened in Florida and Louisiana.

I recognise the protectionist lobby in the United States Congress, but in order to bring about genuine investment in the Caribbean, more will have to be done if the Caribbean Basin Initiative is not merely to be viewed as yet another academic exercise.

Regrettably, the original Caribbean Basin Initiative, which made provision for a 10 percent tax credit to United States businesses setting up in any country in the region, did not materialise. We in the Caribbean perceived this to be a serious short coming of the Legislation and I could only hope that the "great thinkers" in Washington could see the wisdom of reversing what might have made a real difference in terms of channelling investment to our part of the Eastern Caribbean.

I am not a flogger, Mr. Chairman, of dead horses, and will not waste the conference's time on the worn out issues of garments, leather goods, and tax credits. But we have got to learn from the attitudes of the US Congress and throw something in their court. The bottom line for the Congress and Caribbean governments is jobs. That's what protectionism is all about.

We are looking at new industries and new opportunities. The US investor prospecting in the Caribbean, today and in the future, will want to know that when he has a good thing going he does not wake up one morning and hear his Caribbean effort collapse on Capitol Hill. Can we have some minimum guarantee on jobs? If we develop an area, for example, data processing, could we have quotas allocated, not on volumes of trade, but for a certain quantity of jobs? We do not want to put Americans out of work. If Americans are unemployed it is not good for our tourist industry. A thousand jobs in a Caribbean country cannot threaten any billion-dollar industry in the United States. I am therefore suggesting the concept of a Caribbean job quota as a CBI proviso in any protectionist bill. If the Congress of the United States can not fit us into their scheme of things, then they're telling us they regret that the Caribbean exists.

If we cannot break new ground and keep the CBI on steam as a trade package, we in the Caribbean will understand that we are being told to concentrate on tourism. But even here we are back to the constraint of infrastructure where our budgetary resources are limited. Let me say here and now that while we welcome undiminished investment in tourism, and guarantee the repatriation of profits, our islands are too small to accommodate land speculators.

Concluding Remarks:

Mr. Chairman, at the beginning of this presentation I said that I had deliberately stayed away from earlier gatherings of this conference. I am glad I came. But there are two points I want to make in conclusion:

1. I think it pathetic that we all came here to face the US press and public opinion and here we are trying to outdo one another, not exactly washing out dirty linen in public, but every country trying to establish that it has the best bed on which the investor can rest. We hear grandiose speeches about the single destiny of the Caribbean and the Americans but far too many speeches make us look like a Tower of Babel.

2. Many of the presentations do not address the subject.

Furthermore, analysis that should enlighten both the government and the privatesector does not take place. If this trend continues the Miami Conference will loose its significance and not attract meaningful participation in the future.

And finally, let me say a word about the region and my own country. My government has established a credible record of performance in a short time, and no international methods of analysis hold any terror for us. Beyond all the statements made here by everyone about his own situation lie the unwritten words that all discerning critics will discover. We have defined our investment code and the rules of the game in our country. Those of you want to share in our success in management and performance will be welcome. If you care to use my country as a model with which you want to associate, I guarantee that you won't be embarrassed.

The geography of the Caribbean and the Americas provide us with great opportunity. Let us continue to seek the route that will make our history match our geography.

THE REALITIES
OF OUR TIME

*Address at the Fifth
Annual Private Sector
Banquet St. Kitts*

February 28th, 1987

THE REALITIES OF OUR TIME

I do not know what procedures you go through to select your guest of honour for occasions such as these.

I do know what happens to me when I get another invitation to speak from home. The first thing I realise of course, is that before I reach the point of arrival in front of the audience and thanking them for bestowing on me the honour of addressing them, as I do thank you now, I realise that I am letting myself in for more work than I had planned, that I'll have to find the time to settle down and think about my address, and push my body and soul to say enough that will satisfy those who have invited me, and to satisfy the standards I set so harshly on myself.

When last I spoke in St. Kitts at the invitation of your Prime Minister to the Convention of the Peoples Action Movement, I alerted the people of this country to some of the problems we face with the sugar industry in the Caribbean. Those fears have become greater reality in a very short space of time. The end result of these pressures and others like them is that we must think harder than we have ever done before. When we have exhausted all that is possible with the thinking process, we have got to dream and dream again, and be more imaginative than we have ever been, if we are to survive.

One of the terms haunting countries and the international community is "Structural Adjustment". You will hear more and more about it as the realities of your economic pressure strike home. When you hear that it is necessary for your country to go through an exercise of structural adjustment, it means that something is wrong with your economy and you have to make certain corrections.

Now I must turn to the problems of the limits of structural adjustment in the region as a whole.

Whatever the corrective measures accomplished in each of the member territories of the Organisation of East Caribbean States I am still convinced that we cannot do it efficiently, each of us on our own. We did all we could in St. Vincent to reorganise our economy, close the sugar industry, press on with diversification, seek to bring the statutory bodies under fiscal control (a job that is never complete), generate a surplus on recurrent account and all that: However, one tropical storm like Danielle, in half an hour, could throw our adjustment programme out of the window. An instant disaster can strike any of us. You can develop an excellent tourism product in Nevis, but one rape case can emasculate your foreign exchange in an evening. You can get the whole population employed in factories and one line of legislation in the US Congress can put all the people out on the streets.

Together we in these small islands can balance the shocks among us. The hurricanes or economic disturbances do not strike all of us annually; today, it's for me, tomorrow for you. Are we prepared to bear one another's burden? Are we prepared to share our resources, and our knowledge? Are we prepared to move in the direction where our voices will be heard in harmony and unison, or will we be satisfied with the feeble sounds we make on the international stage?

I am satisfied that we are suffering from critical mass in these islands. We just can't do all we want in a small island. We just cannot find or keep all the quality people we want to administer a nation, maintain the technology, and keep the level of service that independence demands.

And while many of you think it is glorious to have the title of Prime Minister, all the glories of that office shrink, when in another country you are asked "How many people do you have in your country?" "What's the size of your place?" And often after you have answered, you get no more questions. People's interest in you shrinks when they realise you are not someone to be taken seriously. And when we are replaced as Prime Ministers individually, the same lesson is therefore our successors, and with the passage of time, even more seriously.

So what are we to do about it?

Imagine how marvellous it would be if we all woke up one morning to find absolute freedom of movement of people, goods, services, and capital in the OECS territories. It would be like a dream. Imagine the opportunities for all of us.

You the people of St. Kitts and Nevis have a wonderful opportunity both with your international airport and the smaller airstrip in Nevis. You are closer to the North American market than a lot of us, also you have an excellent climate. Your beaches in St. Kitts cannot compete with Barbados, Antigua or the Grenadines, but this does not mean that you can not compete in tourism. What you have to do is determine your specific model of tourism and go for it.

The same health trend in the United States that is crippling your sugar industry is what you can go for. People in North America and Europe want health related vacations, with tennis, scuba diving, wind surfing, and fitness clubs. In the not too distant future, the people in the crowed Far East will be stunned to discover how empty are our golf courses. The subscriptions to golf clubs in Japan exceeds the total revenue of St. Kitts and Nevis, and most Caribbean tourist destinations.

But let us not make the mistake in tourism planning similar to what we have made with the sugar industry. We have got to understand the market out there, and in these islands produce the quality of product the market wants.

We need not think for example that because the Japanese produce transistor radios that they would come to the Caribbean to be deafened. I did not hear blaring noises in any city of Japan I visited. Noise pollution constitutes one of the greatest threats to tourism in the Caribbean. And the noise is not really coming from human beings, but from things; the instruments we use to litter the sound waves. The visual images we convey on our posters of natural beauty are negated uncaringly by blasting noises.

And finally, we should not really be aiming to make our countries beautiful for the tourist. We should be aiming at that sense of beauty for our own self, and part of our own culture. So we are not just talking tourism, but social education.

If you are going to move to tourism, and what I am going to say here, applies to my own country as well as others in the Caribbean, we have to make our country more beautiful, make the scenery more attractive, appeal to all the sense and sensitivity, make our own people's attitude more attractive.

I am amazed for example how few are the trees along the avenues in Basseterre and along your roads. This country was not like this four centuries ago. It is human beings who destroyed and exploited the environment, and it is the responsibility of human beings to restore it. We are lucky in St. Vincent that our Botanic Garden was started in 1765 by Captain Bligh and right in our capital city. It might be an idea for this Chamber to start such a project here.

What I am saying therefore, is that the economic structural adjustment that we need individually will only carry us thus far, and will not be enough. Unless the political obstacles of our separate independence are dismantled by the people themselves, the same people will be forever demanding from the system what it cannot deliver. In short, we need a new structure. We need political restructuring.

There is a school of opinion that postulates that Caribbean people are not ready for this, not ready for that, not ready for unity, not ready for the computer programming of a modern society. Some of these opinions find us guilty, and no one is going to get us ready for the various tests of objective critical analysis. It is our responsibility to prepare ourselves, and ours alone.

Every week we spawn a new regional organisation, more and more unbrella outfits, integrating more and more activities, be they in sport, disaster attention, women's affairs, customs administration. On and on the list grows. But in all these efforts to bring Caribbean people together we are still avoiding the basic theme, unity. Cooperation is fine, but the goal of unity seems to be avoided. We slip away from it. We spend more time quarrelling about the pot holes in the streets than the constraints of meaningful development.

As I talk to an organisation of businessmen it is appropriate that I talk in financial terms. Are you, the businessmen in the region, ready to finance the concept of Caribbean Political Integration? Are you ready to look at unification as an investment? Are you sensitive to the market opportunities that will be created in the OECS territories if there is freedom of movement of goods, people, services and capital! Are you ready to throw your weight in the direction for which we really have no serious alternative, or are you going to wait on the population explosion to tell each Government, we have enough protectionism, and see our opportunities shrink rather than expand!

We have got to understand the dynamics of the evolution of forces. If we carry on with our insular independence and all that this implies, we will become even more insular and less economically independent. Everything points to the need for serious re-thinking on unification, be it in business and investment, administration, or the reality of foreign relations.

When will there be an ideal time for this to begin again? Some say we should wait until each territoy has its house in order. That in my view is a recipe for frustration. When years ago Grenada, St. Vincent and St. Lucia met in Petit St. Vincent and organised freedom of movement of our people, in each State the prevailing response was that the crooks from the next island would inundate us. The negative thinking predominates. We are too anxious to be silent on what is good for us, and scream to high heavens about the slightest pin prick.

The leadership of this Caribbean region on the subject of unity has failed us. And I speak not only of the political leadership, but that in the private sector and other fields. The masses do not move leadership, not in China, Russia or South Africa. We have to decide as this century closes whether we as people are prepared to make an act of faith and make a great leap forward toward unity or whether we will continue to crawl, and like a child be only capable of a cry and a whimper!

SHED YOUR TEARS!

*Address at the Opening Ceremony of
the Seventh Conference of Heads of
Government of the Caribbean
St. Lucia*

June 29th, 1987

SHED YOUR TEARS!

It is always a pleasure for me to return to St. Lucia, a place of so many fond memories in my youth. As I retrace those steps I realise such memories are possible, because these islands were all ruled by a single Governor and my step-father came to St. Lucia as a Comptroller of Customs, during the war, some forty five years ago. My mother has been living here since.

My first job in life was teaching Chemistry in St. Lucia, and many St. Lucians, eminent today, passed through my hands. I helped too, in the organisation of a football team which was named the Wolves. I understand that a football team with the same name still exists whose genesis dates back to those early days. It was in St. Lucia too, where I took up my first assignment as an agronomist and diagnosed the difference between nematode infection and potassium deficiency in bananas.

Finally, at the La Toc hotel where our Conference is being held, there still stands some palms which were planted by me. My St. Lucian heritage is indeed very strong! To the people of St. Lucia I say, " *Bonjour, Ca que fait!*"

Mr. Chairman, I wish to join my colleagues in welcoming Prime Minister Ray Robinson of Trinidad and Tobago back into the fold, albeit at a much higher elevation. I was a rather young Trade Minister at a Heads of Government Conference in Jamaica in 1970, when the news came that he had quit the scene. His departure brought that meeting to a premature end. As you know, Prime Minister Robinson, I welcome you not simply formally, but with a real sense of personal pleasure. This Caribbean will always need Trinidad and Tobago, and will always expect firm leadership in that country. I may add, too, that the land of the humming bird was yet another of my Caribbean homes. I have planted trees in Trinidad as well as in Tobago.

I crave the indulgence of our esteemed non-OECS partners if they find I place emphasis these days on OECS union. Even as I do so, I am pleased to remind this audience of the deep philosophical commitment of the MDC leaders to Caribbean political union. We fully understand the reasons why political union with them is not now on our agenda, or indeed on their national agendas. But I want to record that in my own advancement of the cause of East Caribbean Union, I have been encouraged by President Hoyte of Guyana, Prime Minister Robinson of Trinidad and Tobago, the late Prime Minister Barrow of Barbados, and the efforts of Prime Minister Seaga in moulding the Caribbean Democratic Union, which has not been without significance in bringing our parties together. So I know that the entire leadership of Caricom is with their OECS brethren in spirit.

The last time, ladies and gentlemen, that I took to the stage before you was in Barbados, a short while ago, at the funeral of our late beloved colleague, the Right Honourable Errol Barrow. I have been reflecting on that occasion and thinking about what I said (with some embarrassment at the way I said it!) and I have been asking myself: when I too shall have travelled that road, what kind of Caribbean should I have wanted to have left behind? Guided by that fundamental question, I look forward, I re-examine our systems, I endeavour to discern the priorities we must address in the light of the limited time given to us by the Creator. So should we all, and thus define for ourselves the direction in which we want to go.

My scientific training makes me exceedingly sensitive to the fundamental truth about life: that life can never be static. Living things either get stronger, or decline and perish. There is no such thing as a permanent status quo. We the mini-states that are at the bottom of the international pecking order have got to move on in sensible directions, and briskly, if we are merely to survive, let alone keep abreast of the absolute rate of progress elsewhere, which in real terms means advancing at an enormous rate so as to remain no more than where we are.

I have already said quite clearly that I know that the path towards the formation of an East Caribbean Union will not be easy. The only easy posture is to do nothing. We have already gone along another path where we have been telling the people that the answer to their problems is a change of Government. That proposal has its merits, but I am afraid that the changing of Governments which the democratic process provides, or the emergence of dictatorships when the system collapses, obscures the real problems such as the lack of resources, the smallness of size and the restrictions of ecomonies of scale.

First of all, we have to admit to the people frankly and simply, our small size is creating an almost insoluble problem. The roads they want us to fix, the schools and houses and clinics they want us to build, the jobs they want us to create, will all come closer to realisation through union. Many of these legitimate concerns will be addressed. Should we come together, we must understand that if we combine all our budgets, add them all together, the economic strength of the union will be greater than the sum of all its parts. And in this context, the short term expediency of this or that fiscal measure will be rendered less significant if the people have greater opportunity and belong collectively to a single wealthier country.

I do not want to spell out all the details of what kind of union I want, heaven knows, I may have spoken too much already. But I have to borrow a phrase I learned from the great Caribbean Trade Unionist, Tubal Urial Butler; "I am a whole hogger". If we are not talking about a single Ministry of Finance we are joking. If the Union does not speak with a single voice to the international financial community we will not attract the kind of finances we are talking about to fix the roads and houses and hospitals, and to organise the social and physical infrastructure that will launch us into the twenty-first century.

Modern technology today makes available to us certain tools which we can put to use in moulding our countries into a single nation, tools that were not available to the last generation of leaders in the short-lived Federation. I say so, of course, with apologies to the 'Grand Old Man' among us, the Right Hon. Vere Cornwall Bird whose political longevity is one of our Caribbean legends.

Permit me to make brief mention of communication technology. Today, we can speak to each other instantaneously on our modern telephones. Telex, FAX, computers, courier service, better aircraft, more airports, all have created fantastic new opportunities. These kinds of assets are forging new strengths in developed countries and they will consequently be leaving us even further behind in the next century if we do not seize and use the opportunities we now have, opportunities which our fore-fathers would surely have grasped if they were available to them.

Above all, make no mistake about it, we must be prepared to take the leap of faith. Our economists and technicians will, I am sure, provide eloquent answers to all the issues and questions that may arise. But after we have achieved a basic level of understanding in every community, we have got, to have faith in ourselves and our common

107

destiny.

I remember many years ago when as Premier of the Associated States of Saint Vincent and the Grenadines, Premier Bradshaw of St. Kitts, Nevis and Anguilla and I were on the Caribbean team in Brussels negotiating the early concepts of what later became Lome I. We talked about going into independence together. Later, along with St. Lucia and with funding I obtained from the late Dr. Eric Williams, we organised the Wooding Commission on our constitutional future and got it going.

Believe it or not, Bradshaw had recognised that if we achieved independence together, his Anguilla situation would be resolved. And looking at the future of the Caribbean he once said to me, "Son, do you know our West Indian people like to sow today, and reap yesterday!"

I hope we have got beyond that, and are prepared to build for today and tomorrow, rather than leave ourselves as we are.

We must not let ourselves get bogged down at this point in time in too many details. However, apart from the position I have taken on finance we have got to set out clearly the minimum principles of our unification. As I see it, we must have one flag, one anthem, and freedom of movement of people, goods, services and capital. Let us free up the Caribbean and move around as the Caribs and Arawaks did before the Europeans came to the region and carved it up in artifical segments.

Our regional technocrats, in whom I have abundant faith, are capable of producing any legal, constitutional, economic or political structure that we want. Any failure at this time will once more be a failure of the political directorate.

To my colleagues I say, "Don't place yourself on the wrong side of history".

Let me also urge on you the thinking of those of us who have learned the techniques of survival in the smallest islands of our region—the sea faring people of places like Canouan, Petit Martinique and Anguilla and others. Tourism has now added a new dimension to the lives of these people, but traditionally the feeble resources of the land could not sustain them. This Caribbean Sea, that has divided so many of us, for those small island people, is their highway to opportunity.

Mr. Chairman, may I be excused if I respond to the accusation that our initiative is inspired by foreign concerns about their security interests. In so far as my own thinking is concerned, the Caribbean press should know I would be the last person in this region to seek motivation from abroad. My friend Errol wisely decided not to be interred in a grave, for he would surely be turning in it now, if he heard that Son Mitchell was moving in that direction.

My preliminary thoughts on that way forward to unity, as I said in Tortola, have been communicated to my OECS colleagues. Those were my own ideas, intended to stimulate discussion. I did not want to publish those ideas and so give the impression that I have prepared a blueprint. My document has been published, albeit without my authority, but I have no complaints about that because whoever has done so has done me a service, as I am quite happy to allow those suggestions to be used as discussion points. The proposals I have made in that document do not represent a cast iron formula. They have, however, already served the purpose of bringing political union back on the Caribbean agenda, for which I am truly thankful.

In that document I alluded to the increased strategic importance of the East Caribbean if we spoke with one voice for a larger critical geographical area, and how for that reason we will be able to negotiate better financial packages to advance the cause of development of our people. Strategically and geographically we will be embracing the French territories. Also, the Netherlands Government has taken notice of the new atmosphere in the OECS, and I, for one, welcome their interest.

The solid truth of the matter is that the discussions on unity are arguably the most exciting thing that has happened in our region for a long time, and the rest of the world is interested. If these discussions collapse, let me warn you, that like Humpty Dumpty, all the King's horses and all the the King's men, will not put it together again.

What really matters is not any foreign concern but our own enthusiasm. Our OECS initiative must be viewed as a strengthening of the entire integration movement which was supposed to be (unless I have been labouring under a misapprehension all these years) the long term fulfilment of the Caricom dream.

The real imperative, I perceive, is maintaining the momentum on unification. And for Heaven's sake, let me call on you the people to carry the banner. Let me hear the music being played in unison and a discernible melody coming out of every organisation in this region.

We have come from Tortola to St. Lucia. We cannot afford here in St. Lucia not to make progress towards that referendum date. Our next target has got to be the Vancouver Commonwealth Heads of Government Conference and mobilisation of international support in that forum for our programme. Gathering support from the international community must run concurrently even as we move from village to village.

This exercise in fostering unification is fundamental to addressing the wider problems of the Caribbean Community and our declining trade. The fact that intra-regional trade declined by 33% in 1986 over 1985, the largest decline between two consecutive years in the history of the Common Market, is indeed cause for grave concern.

The increasing importance of the OECS grouping as a single market in terms of total intra-regional trade is, I think, by now, well recognised.

Equally important is the continued support of programmes which aim at strengthening the regional market and removing obstacles to free trade; the exploiting of opportunities in Third World countries markets, and the formulating of export development strategies. To this end I welcome the progress made on harmonisation of the customs tariff and on the further development of the Rules of Origin System.

The update of the draft of the Caricom Enterprise Regime is an initiative which we support in principle. Indeed, we view this Regime as a mechanism which would facilitate the development of national and regional enterprises through: (1) the combination of scarce capital and management resources of the region; (2) the promotion of regional ownership and control of priority activities; and (3) facilitating the movement of capital between member countries.

Mr. Chairman I would like to put on record my acknowledgement of the dedicated efforts of the Caricom Secretariat in coordinating the Caribbean Regional Programme under Lome III, which culminated in the signing of the Memorandum of Understanding between the Caribbean—ACP States and the Commission of the European Communities on April 30, 1987 in Dominica. I hope now that the programme has been agreed to by the member countries, we can expect speedy approval from the Commission in order to facilitate the flow of resources back to the region as soon as possible.

Mr. Chairman, as we close this century, in the nineties we will be celebrating the arrival of Columbus, the event that changed this World perhaps more than any other event in World history. Let not the twenty-first century arrive to find the West Indies as politically fragmented as we are today.

As we get ready to commemorate this five hundreth anniversary, I am glad that Spain is in European Community, even though it sends signals which can have serious implications for our banana industry.

Mr. Chairman, ladies and gentlemen, I beg leave to suggest one way in which Europe and North America might commemorate the journeys of Columbus to the Americas, and his outstanding achievements. Let us invite Canada, the United States and those countries of Europe which have had historical links to the Caribbean to put together a development plan for this region, to be called the Columbus Plan. To be launched on the anniversary date of the first landing of Christopher Columbus in this hemisphere.

And finally, ladies and gentlemen, let me conclude as I began, on this OECS initiative. I would pray that at the end of this Caricom Summit here in St. Lucia, we should have harvested the goodwill of our Caribbean colleagues from Guyana to Belize in an appropriately worded statement.

Let us earnestly hope that the day will come when we can honestly tell ourselves and the world: We are a united Caribbean.

I do know, ladies and gentlemen, that some of our people will initially have their doubts. Some might even be a little fearful. With diligent consultation and discussion and public education, our people will be able to fully grasp the beneficial implications of unity.

In Tortola I concluded by leaning on Hamlet, with apologies to William Shakespeare. Here in St. Lucia, I want to conclude by leaning on Mark Anthony. On this subject of East Caribbean unity I urge you, "If you have fears, prepare to shed them now. "

LEADERSHIP AND CHANGE

Address at the Opening Ceremony of the
Authority of the East Caribbean States
St. Vincent

June 1st, 1988

LEADERSHIP AND CHANGE

It is a pleasure to welcome you to St. Vincent and the Grenadines and to assume the responsibility of Chairman of the OECS for this ensuing year.

I welcome you to St. Vincent and intend to ensure that you are also welcomed in the Grenadines. Following the tradition of the other multi-island country where we last met, in the Virgin Islands, I propose to take you to Bequia tomorrow evening so that many of you for the first time will be able to know a bit more about our plural country and so to evaluate the resources about which we speak.

In the last year since Tortola, since the clarion call was sounded placing political unity on the agenda of our territories, the message has been carried into every corner of our countries, willingly or unwillingly, and the theme of our pending goal has gone around the world. We meet this week to review progress and to plan the way forward.

The dialogue on unity has been healthy. Never in the history of constitutional process in our territories has there been so much debate. The debate has certainly been more intense than at independence, and independence was certainly easier to achieve than unity. Independence, in retrospect was a one way traffic with the Imperial Power paving the road, giving us (and our receiving without struggle) the constitution in a fashion that was given to countless others. The process of unification has no single direction, no one power setting out the ground rules. Unification calls for disparate elements to move in the same direction, each in turn giving and receiving, until a new framework is created.

Political progress as we all know calls for setting a time framework. We fixed our Independence dates with Britain, discussed it in Parliament and that was that. We fixed our dates for accession to Carifta and later the Caribbean Community. In my view we will not acomplish unification without fixing a date and working towards it. In Tortola dates were proposed, and those dates haven fallen by the wayside. Have we the courage to fix new dates, or will we let everything slide into limbo?

Whether we like fixing dates or not, we have to adjust to a date fixed by others. The European Economic Community has fixed 1992 as their date for the coming into being as Single European Act. We need to explain this to our people so that they can make comparisons with our own progress or lack of it toward unification, and also adjust to the economic realities that will bear down upon us, whether we are ready or not.

In 1992, all citizens in the twelve European countries that are in the European Community will have common citizenship. They will have absolute freedom of movement. Already passports are being issued in Belgium with the nomenclature that recognises this.

In 1992 there will be airlines deregulation in the EEC which will mean all European airlines will be flying into Martinique, Guadeloupe and Saint Maarten. Martinique is constructing a new terminal building and a queuing ramp for aircraft, in preparation for 1992. What are we doing to get ready for that traffic? Will this external influence instruct us of the need for open sky policies in our territories? For surely, if the Europeans have open skies policies among themselves, and open skies that will include Martinique in the Caribbean, moving millions of people to this region, then surely we are going to look silly restricting movements of a dozen people a day.

We have the destinations in the Grenadines and are getting ready for open sky policies to the Martinique hub, the hub that is the closest to us. And we who have the destinations that people need will continue to offer unrestricted access, in the manner of reciprocity that is universally recognised.

But for heaven's sake let no one assume we will be naive with our generosity.

As this meeting progresses during the next few days, and at its conclusion, our people will be listening to hear whether or not the process of unification has made any advance. They will be listening to hear which of our institutions have been consolidated and which are falling apart. Of course we can all beat the drum of our separate nationalisms and call disunity a victory for realism, and market that response effectively at home. As we lead these countries on the path to unity, as our steps falter on the way, we have to remember the failures of the federation. Standard mythology in the last three decades names the persons whose leadership or lack of it brought down the federation: Nobody blames the Jamaicans or the Trinidadians. They blame Bustamante for his referendum demands, they blame Eric Williams for his "One from ten leaves nought". In this context I want to pose the question "Who among us in the leadership of the East Caribbean is ready for the mantle of failure!" Whether we like it or not, labels of failure to lead the people forward are there awaiting us also.

In our pursuit of unity we find our nationalisms creating stumbling blocks, such as the airline dispute between St. Vincent and St. Lucia, a stumbling block caused by officialdom thinking it can obstruct policy. But all these obstacles that prove convincing to those anxious to find proof of our ill preparedness for unity, to them I say they should look beyond our shores and ask them what restriction is there flying between the islands of the Bahamas, or the islands of Indonesia or the Phillipines? I have said before and I say again that unity demands a leap forward and to leap one must stand, have faith and confidence and move. The alternative is the diffident crawl like a child on all fours and surely we have gone past that, we know where we are going, surely we have the answers and if we don't who will provide them for us!

I do hope we will end up a little better than the troops of the Grand Old Duke of York who: "When they were up they were up When they were down they were down When they were only halfway up They were neither up nor down." My scientific training leaves me with one constant worry about any attempt to stabilise the status quo in the OECS Some would want to say let us consolidate the existing institution before we go any further. Those who would say so would not be aware of the financial chaos in some of the existing institutions, sometimes the staff does not know when it will be paid, as member countries contribution to regional organisations is often at the bottom of their priorities.

In scientific terms, a living body or institution either progresses or retrogresses. The status quo itself is only sustained by progress. To target on simply sustaining the status quo is to target on collapse.

I refer to our leading the people forward, not the people choosing the way. A distinction has to be made between the people exercising democratic choice and leadership providing the areas of choice. To simply say that the matter is up to the people in my view is a way to duck the issue.

The countries traditionally labelled as the great mass movement, China and the USSR are undergoing change. That change is not coming from the people. The Russian revolution too did not come from the people, it came from the intellectuals Marx and Engels and the practical leadership of Lenin. Today it is Gorbachev that is leading the change and in our countries if we the leaders do not lead there will be no change, either. What I am saying to this region is that leadership must provide change. Change will not simply come from the people. It is the same thing happening in the Soviet Union. It takes a Gorbachev to bring change and if Gorbachev fails in the Soviet Union it will be because some other leader emerges to push the country in a contrary direction.

We meet today for the 13th meeting of our OECS Authority. Today one of the most important conferences in the history of the world concluded in Moscow. This morning I watched General Secretary Gorbachev's press conference live on television. The style of that man, what he said and where he is going is something to which in these islands and the Third World will have to pay heed. Let me give you some of his quotes which I copied rather hurriedly". . . "No problem is insoluble . . . . . People are tired of wars and conflicts. . . We are looking for new paths to the future, we are not absolutely right. . . our society is being renewed. . . we must restructure ourselves. . . there is no alternative to *perestroika*. . . the world at large feels that changes might be made. . . today's reality leads us to cooperate. . . the US and USSR must pool efforts and in so doing provide example to others. . . we must expand the limits of cooperation. . . . ." All tall words from a man with the power to change this world. What does it all mean to us in these small islands. We got our independence following on the independence of others in Africa and the Far East because the West did not want those countries under communist influence. Grenada got its airport before the advent of *"prestroika"*. I wonder if they would have got it today! What I am saying is that my perception is that profit for poor countries out of the super power conflict may now have come to an end. I can see greater emphasis will be placed on economic reality, economic strategies of development, and the *"perestroika"* coming out of the World Bank and the IMF.

"Perestroika" will become a word in the English language.

None of us can prophesy the future. What is important is that we perceive the pattern of change and that accordingly we plan constant reassessment of our directions.

In the meantime let us have our Summit in the OECS, send congratulations to President Reagan and General Secretary Gorbachev on their summit.

We can go on and on studying the proposals on unification. We can study this and that to death, we can work out all the intricate mechanisms of furthering trade, deepening integration, running away with sports and so on. In the long run we will come back to the fundamental logic of our geography, our history, the development of our physical and human resources, but above all, we will come back to unification as an idea.

And in stressing unity as an idea, I want to copy the language of the emotive sensual cigarette advertisement on the media frequently heard these days, and in general reference to the importance of the idea of unity to say, "you either got it or you ain't".

A PILLAR OF THE CARIBBEAN IS GONE:
Tribute to Errol Barrow

Oration at the Funeral Ceremony for the Late
Errol Barrow, Prime Minister of Barbados

June 9th, 1987

A PILLAR OF THE CARIBBEAN IS GONE:
Tribute to Errol Barrow

The secret of life, we've found, lies in a pendulum swinging high, swinging low, and truth is sensing when you are swinging high or swinging low: that's my own personal tribute to Errol.

Errol's father and sister were born in St. Vincent. His father the Reverend Reginald Barrow was the priest in my constituency. Perhaps in that ministry was laid the foundation for Errol's own love of sailing, navigation and the Grenadines and our own friendship.

On behalf of my colleagues the President of Guyana, my colleague Prime Ministers and other Caribbean Parliamentarians I say simply: a pillar of the Caribbean Community has gone.

To those of us who succeed him, let us uphold the tradition he has laid. I understand that Errol said recently to his people "hold on". Let us in the Caribbean follow that message; hold on and press on. The Caribbean is one family. Let us in tribute to Errol Walton Barrow continue to build it.

My friend Errol Barrow had a finely tuned sense of elegance in language. I now read for him and for you these lines from Tennyson written over 100 years ago:

Sunset and evening star
And one clear call for me!
And may there be no moaning of the bar,
When I put out to sea,

But such a tide as moving seems asleep,
Too full for sound and foam,
When that which drew from out the boundless deep
Turns again home.

Twilight and evening bell,
And after that the dark!
And may there be no sadness of farewell,
When I enbark;

For though from out our bourne of Time and Place
The flood may bear me far,
I hope to see my pilot face to face
When I have crossed the bar.

WHITHER ANGUILLA

Address at the Inaugural Convention of the
Anguilla National Alliance

July 25th, 1987

WHITHER ANGUILLA

I must thank you very much for inviting me to Anguilla and to address you here tonight. I came here many years ago and met Mr. Webster who was in charge at that time and what I could remember of Anguilla on that first visit is that the roads were all dust clouds. I have watched the development of Anguilla with interest. I represent a constituency in the Caribbean the country of St. Vincent the Grenadines, which is very similar to Anguilla. I have won elections there six times over the last 21 years.

It is rather interesting that in many Caribbean countries, where there are dependent islands, before the quality of leadership in these smaller islands is recognized, absolute chaos has to prevail. It seems a pattern has emerged in these Caribbean States, where out of the Vincentian Grenadines I became Prime Minister of St. Vincent and out of the Grenadian Grenadines, Herbert Blaize became Prime Minister of Grenada (coming from Carriacou,) and the latest to join our fold is Ray Robinson from Tobago to be Prime Minister of Trinidad and Tobago.

We have a similar physical environment to Anguilla and we have similar problems to you. First of all most of our people have traditionally made their money out of the sea, either as seamen, sailors, fishermen or divers: that money has often been made in foreign lands and brought back home to develop our countries. Another similar problem to you is that we very poor rainfall. All of our houses must have water tanks as we do not have a central water supply. We even have a similar type of agriculture, growing corn and peas. Like Anguilla, the islands of Canouan and Mayreau in the Grenadines used to make their living out of producing salt. We have moved away from that kind of subsistence economy becoming mainly dependent on tourism, in addition to our traditional fishing and sailing.

We have in common with you, the people of Anguilla, as a result of that background, and as a result of that dependence on the sea, a rugged spirit of independence. Perhaps it was that framework and that kind of background that led me to hold out for nine years alone in Opposition while all other political parties on the mainland of St. Vincent collapsed. I held out and organised the New Democratic Party which captured and now controls ten of the thirteen seats in St. Vincent and the Grenadines.

We share similar concerns as you in that the seat of government was on the larger territory and the distribution of the revenue from the Treasury concentrated on the constituencies on the mainland. So I know precisely in my representation of the Grenadines the kinds of problems that you in Anguilla must have traditionally faced.

I remember I was once in a political party, before I went out on my own as an Independent, where the Chief Minister at the time told me that there was no money to spend on roads in the Grenadines because the roads in the Grenadines were village roads, and he had not yet got around to fixing villages; he was only working on the main roads. We have come a long way from that kind of condescension.

I have watched with interest the movement towards self-determination in Anguilla, and indeed many of the people in my own constituency have been very jealous of the status that Anguilla enjoys. I do not know if any one has ever told you this, but I am in a position to know, and I am in a position to tell you, of the benefits that went to various parts of your former State of St. Kitts, Nevis and Anguilla. You benefitted by being in control of your own affairs and getting yourself to the position today where you can control your own economic development.

You succeeded 20 years ago because even though you had a very narrow window of opportunity you used it wisely. You are very lucky that things worked out the way they did. At that particular time when Britain was experimenting with Associated Statehood it was a structure that the British Government didn't have much experience with and when you rebelled they didn't quite know what to do.

As a matter of fact, re-establishing Anguilla as a colony was an embarrassment to the British Government and that embarrassment was very ably exploited by the Government of St. Kitts and that is how the Government of St. Kitts secured the building of the Golden Rock Airport. The feasibility study done on the Golden Rock Airport was negative, but so as to try and keep the people in St. Kitts happy, the British Government had to do something for them, even as they were doing something for you, and so the airport was built and Anguilla became a colony again.

In turn, of course, your position has influenced the constitution of Nevis and Nevis itself has been able to work in better and closer harmony with St. Kitts and this has helped both of them to establish and re-establish democracy in that country.

Now, I hope that you, the people of Anguilla, will understand the kind of background from which I address you, and that you understand my sincere concerns for people who have been neglected for a long time, and that they secure their own development in a way that makes their own people happy and improves their quality of life. But from where you are today I would like to share with you some of my perceptions of independence and my perceptions of your own position.

There are not many colonies left in the world today and you have got to bear in mind that colonialism is not a permanent state, no matter how much you would like to keep it, because colonialism is a state over which you alone do not have control. There are two parties to colonialism—the coloniser and those who are colonised—and while you through your democratic processes would have control over public opinion in Anguilla, you will not be supported by public opinion in England forever.

The British Government values today three colonies and I am sorry to tell you that the colonies that they value are: the Falklands, Hong Kong and Gibraltar, not Anguilla. Now you have got to see yourself in that perspective. Sometime we think in terms of a time frame of the next election. There is nothing wrong with that and all of us politicians have got to think of the next election and every parent has got to think of the next meal for the children and so on, but we as leaders, and those of you who are leaders of opinion in Anguilla will have to understand that your planning must be not only for the next election, but for future generations in the next century, and the centuries after that. There is a time when all of us will pass away but the land that God had created will be here forever.

The question is how do we as a people, plan our future, and with these concerns I want to help you understand what is going on in the rest of the world.

You have a very open economy, as traditionally you always have had; you were even smuggling as we smuggled in the Grenadines, and as a matter of fact the smuggling in the Grenadines was also linked to St. Barts. But this brings me the next point. St. Barts and St. Maarten, your neighbours, are creatures of the Dutch Constitution and the French Constitution. So for example, St. Maarten, being part Dutch, part French, and St. Barts, being French, and

Statia being Dutch have a status limited to opinion in the metropolis. These European powers have their own agenda and they have their own political parties and systems, and you the people of Anguilla should not assume that the status of St. Maarten and St. Barts will remain the same forever, from century to century. What will happen in these colonies will depend not only on the thinking in those islands, but the thinking in the metropolis in Europe where there are changing political fortunes as well. Therefore, do not for a moment think that it will not change. You know whence you have come, and of your relations with St. Kitts and Nevis, but the future is something you have got to assess and judge, anticipate and plan for, and you cannot and should not take it for granted.

I want, this evening to open up your thinking on those subjects because even as you have done well you must have some appreciation of what the future may or may not hold. A place like St. Maarten can afford to have the luxury of casino gambling because it works within the framework of Dutch law and security control by the Dutch government. Even though it might just look as though a lot of people are having a good time, the country is developing, and everybody is making a lot of money, there is an inherent strength that you don't see which is the control of the Police, control of the security, and control of defence by the Dutch and French governments. The Dutch government, in viewing the Caribbean, is very sensitive to what is going on* in Suriname, and perhaps because of what has happened in Suriname they might allow the colonial status in these islands to remain a little longer. But I want you; the people of Anguilla, to realise that all these things have a bearing on your life because should Suriname return to democracy and become stable, and things settle down in Aruba and so on, political parties in the metropolis, reviewing these events will come to conclusions beyond your control. You will have to decide in due course whether you remain clinging to St. Maarten and the vagaries of its external control, whether you get caught in the orbit of the American Islands, or whether you gravitate to the English speaking islands.

Now, I do not want to scare anyone, I only want you to recognise some of the facts of life. It may happen that the status of these Dutch and French remain as they are indefinitely; it may happen, but you are a separate country

130

yourself and you will have to decide how you will plan your future for Anguilla on your own or in relationship with your neighbours. You cannot avoid the geography of your neighbours but you will have to consciously assess your own position and determine your future. It is not only a matter of looking inwardly at the jobs and developments in Anguilla, you must also open your eyes to your political environment.

Now let me share with you, ladies and gentlemen, some of our own experience of independence and the difficulties that we are facing, difficulties which are inducing us to think about political union. It was all very nice to put up our own flag, get our own anthem and declare ourself independent, and like everybody else, have a vote in the United Nations. However, it is very expensive to enjoy and exercise that vote in the United Nations. For example, in the OECS territories, every year, in our poverty, we must find an amount in excess of US $500,000 to pay for office rent alone in New York so as to be at the UN; this does not include utilities, telephone, transportation and so on. We find not only that we have that expense: we must also have embassies and ambassadors or representation separately in Washington, in London, at the OAS, and in Brussels. In running these foreign missions and efforts, I am sure we spend a sum which is more than the entire budget of Anguilla—these expenses are duplicated by other OECS members: however, foreign representation is essential if you are going to have contact as an independent country with the rest of the world.

What is more, we cannot afford to do things properly. In the United Nations there are dozens of committees, committees on human rights, on women's rights, committees on economic affairs, committees on cultural affairs, committees on health and so on. We cannot afford, in these small islands, to have more than two or three people representing any one territory. And therefore we cannot afford the expertise, the civil servants or the politicians to man the offices in all those committees, yet that is what independence calls for, and we find that we are duplicating efforts so it is obvious to us that we should try and find a framework to share those costs and to become more efficient and effective. If we were to work together we could use the same money and get more representation in far more countries.

Then there is a question of efficiency in our own administration. With a population about a hundred thousand in each of the Windward Islands we find it very difficult to hire, attract and keep skilled civil servants. You cannot get a first-class civil servant for a salary of less than EC $100,000 a year, similarly, here in Anguilla, in the running of your administration, if you wish to attract quality employees, you have to bear in mind that their abilities allow them the option of working in the private sector, thus the salaries you offer must compare favourably if you wish to attract the right kind of people. We ourselves are finding it a desperate problem, and we have a great shortage of competent manpower. We find also that we need financing for development because the handouts are becoming less and less to countries such as ours. The international community will consider the people of Anguilla wealthy, believe it or not, and you might think that you are poor but when they look at the quality of your houses, when they look at the quality of your services and compare it to certain parts of Sub Sahara Africa and places like Bangladesh you are a wealthy country, and therefore you are not entitled to concessionary aid. That is the nature of the game today, and subsequently we have to be looking for loans on the international market. When we go out to look for those loans we then recognise the problems of our size, the economies of scale, and the scenario of establishing credit worthiness. We have a budget in St. Vincent of around EC $175,000,000. There is no way one of our islands in the OECS by itself can service a loan on a single project of US $25,000,000, and yet we need that kind of money. It is therefore obvious that if we come together and pool our resources, our human resources first of all, in getting the civil servants, the economists and the technocrats working together, they could plan and prepare projects for all the islands as a group, and then we can go and seek the funding. You know the kinds of problems that you have as politicians to try and fix a road to somebody's home and the stress and strains that you have on your limited budget. If we were able to organise ourselves to get that kind of funding it is obvious that we can move equipment from island to island; as you finish one project go to the next and get it done and so on. These are some of the things that we are discovering by way of our lessons of independence and how we ought to be proceeding to get our country developed.

In the pursuit of our development objectives, we have got

to understand also how we are perceived internationally. William Demas gave a lecture in St. Vincent recently, just last Monday night in fact, and he talked about how De Gaulle described us in the Caribbean as "specks of dust". Demas pointed out that at least if we came together we would be a rock. No matter how graciously the representatives of large countries treat those of us who belong to mini-states, when they who represent tens of millions discover that you represent only a few thousand, complete with separate passport and so on, they quietly write you off. They might need your vote occasionally at the United Nations, but that alone cannot sustain our signficance. As in business, respect is conferred by the size of your stock. If we came together in the Caribbean speaking with one voice, the advantages will be greater than the sum of our individual efforts.

One of the facts of life of the geography of our region is that the ships going to the southern United States from Venezuela, Brazil and coming up from the Indian Ocean under South Africa and so on, all pass through our waters. Access to the Panama Canal from the Mediterranean and from the Atlantic passes through our waters. We live in a very important geographical area and this area has been important since the time of Columbus, important for other people who explored, discovered, and controlled the new world, and that significance of our position has not yet diminished. It does not mean that we have some asset that we should abuse in negotiation with those who appreciate our strategic location, but all I am saying is that we have something that we should appreciate, and that we should understand our position, maximise our geography through unity, and work in harmony with other countries that control this hemisphere of ours for our mutual benefits.

If we unite from Anguilla in the North, to Grenada in the South, and become a single archepelagic state, we will not only have a modicum of members to attract respect, we will be controlling access to the Panama Canal, controlling a wider strategic area and be able to negotiate a better deal for ourselves from the international community. Speaking now with single voices we are not heard.

In contrast with these grandiose perspectives, we in these mini-states operate a democracy that is very fragile. We are engaged in the business of development and so we not only have to negotiate with foreign investors and with foreign

133

governments, but we also have to tend the shop and look after our people, and the gutters in the villages. And while the governments in these small islands may have the most grandiose plans, the most well-intentioned plans are often subject to change.

When you have an electorate of 150 votes as you do here in Anguilla, if you quarrel with one family you could lose the elections. If you don't give the right fellow the job on a garbage truck the government could fall. If you stop some youngsters from kicking a football in front of an old lady, you could lose the seat also.

Now when we talk about democracy we must understand the critical problem of our small size, and the anguish that we have trying to keep on track. Where you could be carrying your people almost the full mile but because you don't carry them the last inch they want to say you are the worst man or woman in the world, and our people, due to their lack of experience of government, or their limits in education, do not put things into the broad perspectives. Our democracy is a very difficult thing to maintain with a very small electorate; and when you put in balance the targets of development that you want to get for your people, you might have an elected representative who is quite capable of negotiating for the best deal on an electrical generator which in turn will mean a low tariff on your electricity, but you might find the electorate rejecting that person in preference to someone else whose only asset is that he makes a good showing at Carnival. These are some of the problems in our small societies and quite frequently when you look at it you can see how dangerous these factors are in trying to lay the foundations for the future. These are all critical things which we all need to assess and analyse because if you are trying to talk about the future of Anguilla there are some genuine and real problems that can set you back for a long time as you try to go forward. These issues facing us are what I call fundamentally structural problems inherent in the politics of a small community.

You find, for example, that because of remoteness you may receive revenue by sale of exotic postage stamps. But in dealing with stamp merchants, do you have the level of expertise to understand what is going on in the philatelic world? Do you have the level of expertise to negotiate? We discovered our weakness in St. Vincent and so did other Caribbean territories. You find yourself dealing with a company in England and one day you get a telex saying the company went bankrupt and, before you look around you have lost several million dollars. You get involved in dealing with offshore banks: do you have the technology or financial and fiscal management to really understand what is going on and to stop experienced investors from exploiting your innocence. Have you got the accountants who are capable of understanding, and do you have sufficient numbers of honest people to tell you when something is going wrong? The question is how does a small country with a weak tax base secure the expertise necessary for running a government. You are small as we are small in St. Vincent and the Grenadines—we might be a little bit bigger than you, but on that world scene out there, we are very small, and we must face the constraints of our size. My good friend, the deputy Prime Minister of Antigua, went to China the other day and I asked him, "When the people in China and Shanghai and Canton asked you about the population of Antigua, what did you tell them?" He said, "I told them I am from the Caribbean, with five million people".

Apart from the constraints we allow our history to impose on us in the political isolationism we deploy, we face external threats from the drug barons. My colleagues have told me how President Lusinchi of Venezuela has expressed fears for Venezuela dealing with the resources of the drug barons, now diverting routes from Panama to his country. If oil rich Venezuela, a land with abundant resources fears the drug trade, what are the chances of a small island such as yours with ten thousand people of coping!

In this scenario what are our prospects in this region for security and long term stability, each of us, sovereign and alone? We are peaceful, blissful, in these small islands, but bear in mind there are lots of people who would not hesitate to exploit our serenity, our simplicity and our cool way of going about things. They will not hesitate to do so at all; and some of our people will not hesitate to take the easy drug money if they can get it and so we will lose control of our society. So our stability is very much in question, facing those kinds of problems. If you for example, develop a drug problem, as the Turks and Caicos Islands developed sometime ago, you will only wake up one morning and find out that the UK has suspended your constitution. These are the realities of colonialism; you may ignore these things, but these are the limits within which you operate.

Ladies and gentleman what I am trying to establish is the difficulty in maintaining effective control of our countries. Such are some of the reasons why we are talking seriously about coming together in the Eastern Caribbean. Some of our countries feel that they are doing very well and everything is going all right for them, so they do not have to bother with unification, but in my view that position is very shortsighted. Our Caribbean region is one that has known a history of boom and bust.

Once upon a time cotton was king and we made a lot of money out of that crop but today cotton has vanished. Once upon a time sugar was king, now sugar is a pauper; once upon a time spices and indigo made the Caribbean famous; that is no longer the case.

We see in regard to our tourism that we have peaks and troughs. You have seen even places like Paris be shaken security concerns with a single bomb blast in a railway station. One bad incident here in Anguilla, blown up in the press in the United States, and your tourism will be finished for several months. These are real problems when you have an economy that is dependent on a single source. Look at Trinidad. A few years ago Prime Minister Williams was boasting: "Money is no problem". Tonight as we gather here, Trinidad is short of $2 billion on its balance of payments. So during boom times, some countries in the Caribbean will say, "Oh, we are alright; our economy is bounding along," but when the collapse comes, the language of Caribbean Brotherhood surfaces again.

I was delighted when I heard your Chief Minister make reference to your planning and controlling the level of your development here in Anguilla. What you need is to make sure that everybody here makes a good living and has a good life, but you must understand that it is not necessary for you in Anguilla to have so much development that you need to bring into Anguilla more migrant workers that the Anguillan people themselves. You should assess the optimum level of first class hotel rooms you require to give you full and balanced employment, how many you require for reasonable economic growth, and settle at that level. Other wise your country will be swamped, your identity submerged.

I am pleased to be here with colleagues in the Caribbean Democrat Union to help you organise this first political

136

convention, and help you organise your party structure. When this is done we will welcome you into the Union.

I wish to congratulate you on the progress you have made since you re-established your identity some twenty years ago. I want to assure you that the new ideas we are exchanging in the Caribbean on political union create new opportunities for all of us. My constituency is no different from yours. You too can help fashion the structure we hope to create. Opportunities will be there for you and your leaders in the new Institution we hope to create. I know the traumas you in Anguilla have had in the past. We in the Grenadines have suffered too. When the time comes that you have to move on, remember that we in the English speaking Caribbean will always have a place for you and a door open for you.

*The military control by Commander Bouterse.

VILLAGES IN THE SAME VALLEY

*Address at the Fifth Symposium of
the National Library of Aruba*

September 7th, 1987

VILLAGES IN THE SAME VALLEY

I wish to thank the Prime Minister, the Honourable J.H.A. Eman, and the National Library of Aruba for inviting me to present my views on our Caribbean region at this Symposium. I am delighted that the news of our ongoing effort at political union in the East Caribbean has evoked your interest. It is significant that as you review and plan your own future in Aruba, that you should want to evaluate trends in the Caribbean basin which we all share.

I bring greetings to the people of Aruba from the people of St. Vincent and the Grenadines. Many are the older citizens in our country who have fond memories of their Aruba days in your oil refineries, and who are still grateful to you for the economic foundation which opportunites in these Dutch Antilles laid for them. Indeed, but for an accident on one of my family schooners I may have been born in Curacao. My father sailed here regularly and one of my uncles had his first job here. One of my Ministers was in fact born in Aruba during the Second World War: a number of our young men perished on the way to Aruba on a ship that was shelled. The list of our historic linkage is long. A number of our Prime Ministers and Ministers in the East Caribbean worked as young men in these Netherland Antilles and that is an experience on which we should draw in cultivating our relations today.

May I now take this opportunity for the very first time since we in St. Vincent and the Grenadines are independent, to thank you, the people of the Netherland Antilles, for the help you gave our people in the past.

This help which you gave with your own human resources, compared with the economic pressures you faced because of the recent downturn in economic activity in the oil sector, provides an example of the swing in our Caribbean fortunes. The Caribbean seems to be constantly going through periods of "boom and bust". This phenomenon over the decades is certainly one which we must all appraise. We all need to evaluate the experience of each other, in particular when we are on the upswing. Had Trinidad and Tobago studied the downturn in Aruba a few years ago when they were in their "money is no problem" phase, they would not be into the horrors of a deficit on the imbalance of payments today. I wish to congratulate the people

141

of Aruba on the smooth transition you have made in structural adjustment from the oil economy to tourism. Not many other parts of the Caribbean would take a 25% cut on all wages without a riot.

Experience should teach us that the peaks may be sharp but the troughs are long. We need therefore to devise strategies for soundly based continuous economic growth (and employment). That kind of stability cannot materialise only through economic and fiscal management. The bottom line is political, and the fundamental thrust has got to be constitutional.

As we plan the future, one of the things we should guard against is what I mean by the platitude, "trying to re-invent the wheel". We can learn a great deal from the experience of others, and what is taken for granted in certain advanced countries can appear imaginative or even revolutionary if applied in our cases. For example, France and Germany are miracles of economic recovery since the last war, but they had to refashion their institutions, particularly their constitutions, and it is that political restructuring that paved the way for their economic recovery and world leadership today. They have relatively new systems functioning in very experienced civilizations. All too often in our planning in this part of the world we are bogged down by standpipe politics, and while I recognise the essential importance of satisfying the immediate demands of our people, if we the leaders think we will satisfy the macro economic perspective by fixing one standpipe after another and not encompass the wider possible vision, our people will be bucket fillers at the standpipe forever.

You the people of Aruba might want to know why those of us who are now independent, with seats in the United Nations, embassies in the capitals of the world with flags on the limousines of our ambassadors, should want to change our status when independence per se should be the final constitutional product of colonialism. So why these new thrusts in the East Caribbean.

The truth is that sovereign independence demands economic independence. And we are discovering that we can't make it very well. None of us can afford to rent, let alone own, our own building for an embassy in New York, Washington, Ottawa, London, Paris, Brussels, Rome, Scandinavia, Africa, The Middle East and Central or South America. We are all in New York and at the United Nations

and little else. There ought to be a basic threshold of assertion of independence, and if we can't keep up now, it will
only get worse in the future. And while we are all in the
United Nations Assembly, we all vote the same way anyway,
and when we don't, as happened with Grenada or Afghanistan, we only make fools of ourselves. While we can take
part in the General Assembly we do have limitations with
the number of committees and agencies we can service. Instead of all of us asserting our independence in the same
forum, or in the same city, united we could spread our
wings and show the flag in most places. We are a maritime
community, and the international community has difficulty
dealing with us. Only France has an embassy in any of the
East Caribbean territories. Foreign countries grace us usually
with non-resident Ambassadors. So Germany deals with us
out of Port-of-Spain, the US out of Bridgetown, Israel out
of Jamaica, Austria out of Caracas and so on. The British
grace us with a Deputy mission, and Taiwan and Venezuela
with a Charge d'Affaires.

In turn, independent countries that wish to grant us economic assistance find that they need to deploy too many
officials to deal with too small numbers. Their own administration in assisting us would be more efficient if we were
united and it is obvious that we would be the beneficiary.

But lest I give you the impression that it is external concerns of ours and others that motivate our thrust to unity
let me tell you some of the weaknesses inside.

We have established a high level of functional cooperation
inside the East Caribbean in the grouping called Organisation of Eastern Caribbean States, including the BVI, Anguilla, St. Kitts and Nevis, Montserrat, Antigua, Dominica,
St. Lucia, St. Vincent and the Grenadines and Grenada.
This order lists us geographically, north to south. There is
a fruitful mechanism also in the wider Caribbean Community that embraces Belize, the Bahamas, Jamaica, Barbados, Trinidad and Tobago and Guyana.

The functional cooperation brings various Ministries,
Departments and organisations together to plan joint
strategies of development, and there is now hardly a week
going by without a regional meeting taking place. These
meetings, for example, include separate gatherings of Tax
Administrators, Statisticians, Comptrollers of Customs,
Fishery Officers, Agricultural Officers, all levels of medical
personnel, police, and so on. There are mechanisms for

meetings of various Ministers, in various portfolios: Finance, Foreign Affairs, Health, Transportation, Trade, Agriculture and so on. And to tell you the truth, there is hardly anything being discussed in the entire region that one person and one administration could not deal with. In the East Caribbean we have a single Central Bank and an Eastern Caribbean dollar. To date it has served us well. Our currency is well backed with more than adequate reserves and resources, and our only constraint on the high value of our currency is our competitive disadvantage in trade.

This functional cooperation, particularly in dealing with the international community, has shown us how much greater will be the advantage if we spoke with a single voice. Working together we have impacted on the decisions of the World Bank, seeking to graduate us from concessional financing, and thereby secured a temporary respite. In dealing with the European Community we secure better protection for our bananas, and a better package of economic assistance for the region than we could have done if we were negotiating alone.

But there are stresses in the functional cooperation. Some people don't pay their bills. In periods of economic recession, the last bill to be paid is the one outside your country. The limited number of foreign missions, like the regional institutions, do not seem to be a high priority for our governments. This in turn affects the human resources at our disposal.

The human resource factor in each individual country is under pressure. It is becoming increasingly difficult to attract and retain the level of technocrats at home which we require for our development as independent countries. In the colonial days we did not need resource personnel to deal with the World Bank, the International Monetary Fund, the Food and Agricultural Organisation, or other United Nation Agencies. And it is critical that one copes in this area, otherwise your country rating is not properly done and the flow of resources from the international community, essential for development, is retarded.

Of course, the level of perception of these and other issues in our region varies. Some who are still colonies are not aware of these problems. Some who are independent have a different agenda.

Essential in all this is an understanding of the framework of time. First of all one has got to be capable of evaluating the level at which one's country is at, and the rate of progress and the kinds of progress happening in the rest of the world. We are a long way behind and sometimes do not know that we ought to be busy seeking to escape the emotional arrogance of our chauvinism. Several opportunities we have already perceived are going begging because we are not in a position to seize them. The minimum threshold of serious international understanding on a single project is US $25 million. With an annual island budget of say US $60 million to provide all our goods and services there is no way we can take up such a loan. But with a total budget of approximately US $250 million we can collectively take on this kind of loan for multi-projects in various islands, be they in roads, jetties or other infrastructural demands. Efforts in these directions will break the recurring cycles of our poverty.

One school of opinion is that we should be perfectly organised before we unify, but I am afraid this will never happen. Development is a process and we have constantly got to seek means of restructuring our systems. The fundamental problem for our island governments is one of critical mass. We suffer from it daily in the problems of our Administrations. Our slender resource base can hardly accommodate the cadre of professionals we need without distorting the salary structure in our civil service. All these ongoing internal economic problems indicate the need for political restructuring.

There have been many, up to very recently, who postured as Caribbean integrationists with flowery speeches on the inevitability of our common destiny, who have silenced themselves now that the idea of political union is firmly on the agenda. Their posturings are finished for all time. They hoped that they could preserve their sacred status indefinitely while functional cooperation will merge into political union. William Demas, the scholarly President of our Caribbean Development Bank has seen through this and stated quite firmly that functional cooperation has never lead and will not lead to political union. Both functional cooperation and political union need separate acts of political will.

And now I will turn to my perception of Aruba, Suriname, the rest of the Netherland Antilles and your possible relations with the English Speaking Caribbean. This context will in turn overlap our concerns with the French Antilles and Latin America.

In Anguilla, I recently touched on these subjects, explaining to the people of that colony that with the withdrawal of British responsibility in this region, they will one day either have to gravitate towards the Netherland Antilles or be more involved with the English Speaking Caribbean. When I speak like this some people who can only think from day to day do not realise that I am taking a long view of history. With the Europeans themselves moving to establish a passport marked European Community on its cover with a subtitle of the country of citizenship, where will we then be with separate identities in the Caribbean in another ten years, let alone five or six decades.

What I was telling the Anguillans is that they are riding piggy-back on the St. Maarten economy which is a figment of the Dutch and French Constitutions. Opinion among political parties in the Netherlands and in Europe in general changes. The question is: Do we in the Caribbean wait for opinion in Europe to change and perhaps leave us stranded, or do we plan our destiny for ourselves? I was Premier when the Bank of England terminated the guarantees on our Eastern Caribbean dollar without choice. When we went to London to discuss it, we got a lovely lunch. That's all! The closure of your oil refinery or a new line in a law in the United States on taxation, demolishes your economy. This is the painful lesson of the small open vulnerable economies that we are. We have got to have these islands' constitution restructured for our economic salvation so that the stroke of someone else's pen does not leave us stranded. We must digest these lessons or perish.

While Suriname has drifted away from the democratic ideals, I expect there will be no thrusts from Europe toward constitutional evolution in the Netherland Antilles, but one day Suriname will be back to normalcy, and your scenario in these islands will change. This will be healthy.

We have, since independence, a very health relationship with the European Community as defined in succeeding Lome Conventions. We have also smooth relations with the United Kingdom Government, but one of the real constraints in the furtherance of our economic relations comes right back to the limitations of our human resource personnel to extract all we can out of the economic agreements. We were allocated five million pounds grant and five million pounds loan since Independence year, 1979. We are only now about to begin to draw down our loan funds in 1987. There is much evidence of our administrative limitations.

I am quite satisfied that the Europeans do not want colonies in the Caribbean. Some, like France, are quite happy to remain integrated with the Caribbean or hold a referendum on independence should the people of any territory so desire.

Our greatest problem remaining in the region is our need to find out whether we want to remain where we are, or whether we want to advance. In any event, it is up to us to define a strategy on our future. If we have to keep our linkage with the Europeans, then we should both be thinking about the subject. Things should not be left to drift. Mere acquiescence in the status quo, in my opinion, is very useless, and serves neither our interest nor theirs.

It is rather insulting to us as Caribbean people that we should hear that the departure of the Europeans leaves a power vacuum in our hemisphere. Do you want to tell me that those of us descended from Europe, Africa, and India are here and we constitute a vacuum?

If we can't marshall our intellect and our forces to constitute a region to be respected internationally then we deserve the contempt which the statement about "vacuum" engenders. In my view, some independent countries, in the way they go about their business, are creating a greater vacuum.

The plain unadulterated truth is that a small country with 100,000 people cannot make much of an impression by itself in the international community. You can accomplish notoriety—as did Grenada by being a pawn for other interests, by becoming an irritant. Everyone knew about the communist threat in Grenada, challenging the security of our hemisphere; but who knows or cares now about the fiscal deficit and the anguish it causes there now. And the problems which we have are fundamentally our own, that of the small size of our resource base, and the huge appetite of our people fed on an international culture by satellite, and without the supplies coming by satellite.

But in my view the Grenada experience, its communist capture by a few men, and the inherent weakness of the system in a small country, all inform the leftists in our region that political unity must be restrained at all costs. My politics of the centre, where I concern myself with the priority of economic and social development, rather than spending a fortune on arms or defence, my distaste for a regional army, the left wing could accept. But the unity which I propose, again based on Economic and social necessity, that carries in its train a single police force, becomes anathema to them, for they begin with their socialist premise where nothing must endanger their "historic" opportunity. Economic and social development and self reliance in our region will not allow the chaos on which communism will thrive. And those who think that emphasis ought to be placed on military security by itself, without speedy attention to the people's needs, are equally short sighted, in my view. I only hope that the people of Grenada will all understand the quest for unity in the context. If they go wrong, I don't know who will rescue them again. There will not always be a Reagan in the White House.

Out of my twenty-one years in leadership in my country, the experience gained with addressing our needs, assessing the orientation of the international community toward small states, I am abundantly satisfied that we need political union in the East Caribbean if we are to survive into the twenty-first century. Power is becoming more and more concentrated. For their own progress the Europeans understand it clearly. The evidence is on our transistor radios all the time. You hear it in the trade wars on cereals and manufactured goods, the fight against drugs and terrorism. But all these lessons our people will not grasp by themselves. The responsibility for new directions will always remain with leadership.

We in the Caribbean are all villages in the same valley. We need to pool our resources and so overcome our separate and several limitations. The brightest and best intellects in our region see the problems and answers quite clearly.

One fundamental ingredient of our separate sovereignty in the Caribbean democracies is that with separate governments we each have elections each year. Elections, by themselves, even without paying attention to results, produce uncertainty. At least if we had fewer governments we would have fewer elections. If our islands had a single government then there would obviously be a single election. This would produce more stability in those islands. Stability will enhance confidence, and confidence will in turn stimulate investment and economic growth, thereby providing opportunity to deal with problems such as unemployment, for example.

The real secret of foreign relations today is not assertion of separate sovereignty but rather finding the means to use the tools of independence, to maximise the well-being of your own people. The resources that need to be deployed are formidable. We don't have those resources and we have to rely on the genius of a very few people.

Now let me tell you what is going on, on the ground in the East Caribbean. Two speeches, quite unconnected, by William Demas of the Caribbean Development Bank in June 1986, and mine in Tortola in May 1987, were what initiated the current dialogue on unity. Demas' ideas were put forward to the region in general, but never discussed by the Prime Ministers. In September 1986, I raised the issue of political union among my colleagues and they requested I put forward a paper. I did so in the following October, and my ideas were basically appreciated. But it was not until the call for action with two referenda on the subject was made in my Tortola address that unity came forcefully on the political agenda.

The reason for the two referenda is straight forward. The Prime Ministers, who are interested in Union, do not want to proceed without knowing in principle that the people are interested. It makes no sense drafting a constitution for unity when people want to preserve the status quo and want to cultivate their insular prejudices until all eternity. The second referendum, if we get to that stage, will be a constitutional necessity, for approving the new constitution. Such is the procedure agreed by the Prime Ministers for consultation with the people. The second referendum will not take place if there is not the first, or if the first is not positive.

The process of education and consultation is underway.

One of the reasons why unity is on the agenda now and has not been for a couple decades is that we in the leadership today are very close. We think alike. We have all had two decades of experience. We know the limits of the so called glamour of Prime Ministerial status and are quite prepared to shed it. I am afraid that some of the opposition to unity stems from those who dream of that glamour of status as a lifelong ambition, and others (not only in politics) who want to preserve the familiar. I am yet to be convinced that there is an argument in the familiar. I am yet to be convinced that there is an argument in the interest of our people that does not support political union. Heaven knows I care too much about the union to sound arrogant, but a single traffic accident affecting the lives of any of our present dedicated leaders will bring the thrust to unity to a close. If and when it is established, leadership will not be that critical.

I know that there has been no better time for unity than exists today. I know the forces to be overcome today and in the future. Those who appeal to go slowly and who are not prepared to think their way to the solution, knowingly, are aiding and abetting failure for the unification process. If we fail now, it will not happen again. The functional cooperation of which we boast will not improve: it will collapse.

So at this point of time, I regret I cannot prophesy to you the people of Aruba what the future of the English Speaking Caribbean will be like. Whatever happens, it is obvious that the Netherland Antilles and ourselves should develop closer relations. We all must plan to work closer with the Latin America that surrounds the Caribbean basin. To do this our people in greater percentages must have the communication tools in language. Our countries must have better transport linkages. There is much to be done as we look outward and around. But the first priority is to get our houses in order, and establish the systems that create imaginative opportunity.

I am sure I speak for all the Caribbean when I say that we in the English Speaking Caribbean would certainly wish to improve and develop our relations with the Netherlands Antilles or those who were former Dutch colonies. We have moved from colonialism to independence, from chauvinistic insularity to a new awareness of the limitations of our internal resources and the constraints on our external relations. Many are the experiences in foreign relations we can share with you who aspire to independence. If our unity succeeds, there will be greater momentum in our region and we will be in a position to work ever more meaningfully with you. If more of us speak for the Caribbean with a single voice, the better it will be for all of us. The rest of the world knows and perceives the Caribbean as an entity. It will be always a constant struggle to inform the world about Aruba or St. Vincent. The Caribbean identity is still there waiting to be captured by the Caribbean people.

Part II

STRATEGIES

OF

DEVELOPMENT

WHAT KIND OF CARIBBEAN
DO WE WANT?

*Paper presented at the Symposium "Societies
of the Caribbean: Development and Security",
at Seven Springs Center, Mt. Kisco, New York.
Policy options related to President Reagan's
Caribbean Basin Initative*

March 1982

*This speech, written while the author was in
the St. Vincent parliament, was read into the
United States Congressional Record on
April 5th, 1982.*

WHAT KIND OF CARIBBEAN DO WE WANT?

Not since the Churchill-Roosevelt deal exchanging destroyers for land bases has there been any serious US planning in the Caribbean. Once more security brings the US-Caribbean relationship into focus; President Reagan has announced the Caribbean Basin Initiative. In 1940 the enemy was clearly distinguishable, and equally recognised to be such, both by the Caribbean and the United States. In 1982, however, although the US may be single-minded in its position, the Caribbean with its political diversity cannot agree on a common enemy.

The recent decades of separate independence, and all the opportunities missed at political union, have created the opportunity for multiple sovereignty and in turn the right of the various Caribbean states to conflicting foreign policies. Although under the umbrella of the Caribbean Community there is the pious hope of foreign policy coordination, in fact, this has been confined to securing trade preferences or jobs for the boys in the international agencies. Many a plenary session of a Caribbean Foreign Ministers' meeting will issue a grand communique' on a common position, but in practice Ministers are quite capable of striking their country's bilateral deal in private, much to the embarrassment of foreign governments dealing with the Caribbean. A lot of time and effort can be wasted in trying to help the Caribbean if from the outset this insularity is not recognised. President Reagan's Caribbean Basin Initiative must therefore first of all come to terms with the heterogeneous nature of the sovereign states in the region, and their conflicting priorities.

Lest the underlying intention of the Caribbean Basin Initiative is to maintain the status quo in the Caribbean. I would like to point out that the status quo in the Caribbean is one of poverty. To talk therefore of maintaining the status quo means to advocate reinforcing poverty. Policies of assistance to these islands must therefore guide change, or at least encourage the need for change. Sustaining the rule of political parties resistant of change merely postpones the resulting conflict. The political parties of the center seeking orderly change are the natural allies of a self-confident America, and not those imposing so-called stability on a starving population.

The low economic level of the vast majority of our people

remains the basic problem. Massive financial assistance is essential. But merely pumping money in will not of itself improve matters. The Caribbean Basin Initiative will be mainly money down the drain if the inherent weaknesses of the region, and the specific problems of each state are ignored.

Corruption and incompetent administration steadily consume huge portions of well-intentioned aid money; but I propose to discuss some of the other factors which drastically diminish the value of aid.

The population explosion negates many of the hard-earned tax-dollars poured into the region. Our population is doubling every twenty years. Can any of us really cope with a Caribbean population twice its present size by the turn of the century? Barbados, the citadel of common sense in the Caribbean is the only island that has announced, and proudly, nil population growth. Unfortunately the announcement of such a target in many islands could trigger a riot.

In projecting the quality of life desired in the Caribbean we must have the courage to ask the question: just how many people can these islands accommodate? Will St. Vincent with a per capita income of EC $250 for 115,000 people be able to cater for 230,000 by the year 2000? How can we cope with a country in which 50% of the population is under 18 years and 30% of the babies are produced by teen-age mothers who do not even own their own bedroom?

The arguments about population control have been voiced time and time again, but as long as the problem exists, policy planners will have to come back to it, and it is important that we the policy makers spell out the problem clearly. We cannot expect others continually to pick up the bill for our indifference.

Finite resources cannot satisfy infinite growth. Oil crisis, lesson one. Other lessons like phosphate shortages for food production are waiting in the wings. And as elsewhere in the developing countries any development strategy for the Caribbean that excludes an ingredient of population planning will be doomed to failure. Nor will seminars for the elite be enough. Birth control appreciation has to be part of basic education that functions within the framework of enhanced economic opportunity. Wealthy Roman Catholics the world over ignore the Pope, and the problem is left with the uneducated poor. Poverty bring instability which brings repression and States of Emergency. Religious fanatics who oppose birth control support the imposition of States of Emergency and all the evils which come under that heading.

Next, the brain drain! The massive capital required for our recovery needs talent for conversion into growth. When the people who know how to make money work have vanished, recovery will be slow. The tragedy of Jamaica today is the loss of talent in the last decade. The executives, and the plumbers whose children are now at school in Miami will not return home to start reorganising their family life. The confidence they lost in their country will not return after one election.

But above all it is the constitutional fabric in which our islands are insuitably clothed which is the basic impediment to improvement of our low productivity. Transported Westminster is not working in these islands. Indeed Roy Jenkins of Social Democratic fame in Britain has enunciated in in his Dimbleby lecture how the Westminster system is partly responsible even in Britain for industrial decline. No country has articulated more clearly than the United States the belief that productivity is tied to the political system. I agree. Extensive capital investment will not create self sustaining growth in an unproductive political system, be it in Poland or Haiti.

The constitutional systems in these islands befell us while America, languishing in Vietnam psychosis, allowed Britain to excuse herself from the problems she had created on America's doorstep. I know that American diplomacy deliberately left the islands up to the British, while Britain concerned itself with abandoning the islands. Our roads were abandoned, and so were our schools. Our health services in the Windwards do not match those of Martinique between us. Thus the United States must pick up the tab for American contributary negligence over the last two decades.

Stable government, it is said, is the real basis for economic growth. But stability cannot be derived from a system that establishes a government whose authority derives from a minority of the population. That system works in Britain where strong traditions have prohibited the unthinkable, where check on maladministration through the Press, the Courts and Public Opinion are as strong as the Government itself. Not so in a small island where Government is the main employer, the main dispenser of patronage and the guardian of opportunity. And the financially eroded Press barely exhibits a shadow of the truth. The minority government becomes paranoid, and it becomes for example a legal offense, (and here I quote from the draft St. Vincent Public Order Act) "to have an intention to bring into hatred or contempt, or to excite disaffection against the government. " Furthermore, persons are to be detained who are suspected of have an intention of being about to commit an offense.

Foolish legislation, however 'legal', can be a prime cause of instability. Authoritarianism sponsored in this fashion prescribes economic chaos. Criticism is an essential nourishment for the healthy growth of a society. When laws prevent criticism we inherit the infertile territory of callousness.

Without safeguards the Westminster System allows a minority to legislate themselves into an authoritarian regime. Effective participation of substantial areas of the population can be silenced. In the 1980 Trinidad elections the ONR party received 84,000 votes and no seats in Parliament, while the Alliance Parties won 83,000 votes and 10 seats. In the 1979 St. Vincent Election opposition parties secured forty-six percent of the vote and two out of thirteen seats, thereby providing the government with a two thirds majority capable of ammending the constitution at will. Including those who do not vote the mandate for the government was a mere 34% of the electorate!And St. Vincent's record shows this type of power used to make the wife of a Government Minister the Leader of the Opposition!

It is within this framework of authoritarian tendencies that one must be cautious in defining security needs. Experience of Guyana has taught that defense expenditure, like elsewhere in the Third World is not directed at the external enemy, but at the citizens themselves, especially on election day.

But however repressive a regime becomes in the preservation of its own power it may be overthrown—witness the Shah of Iran and the Emperor of Ethiopia. Likewise an unworkable constitution cannot be assumed forever inviolate. Much of Africa has had to adapt to new constitutions to forge their developmental needs. France with its centuries of self reliance has found a new formula in our lifetime. Indeed the French model of ensuring that the government represents more than 50% of the electorate is a principle we should emulate. Nor should we forget the chaos out of which the Fifth French Republic was born. And we too should be allowed to evolve our appropriate constitutions in the attempt to bring sanity to our plural heritage.

Nor will we necessarily secure the formula for stability with one thrust. Trinidad and Tobago is a case in point. Not long ago exhaustive consultation produced the Republican formula, but the sudden profusion of oil wealth has created a new round of confusion. Autonomy for Tobago has pointed to the need for decentralisation in Trinidad itself.

The heady rhetoric of self determination was supposed to come to an abrupt halt when the Indepence flags were hoisted, even though several elements in the society remained adrift in a sea of selfishness. Decentralisation is construed to be a threat to rulers. A free vote for autonomy is unpatriotic. But self determination is and will be a continuing process and can only be said to be realised when people enjoy a constitution that fulfils theirs lives.

The theory is put forward that autonomous territories will fall prey to Cuba or the Mafia as they are too small to manage themselves. But autonomists are not unmindful of the Cuban guns constantly hammering the hungry Eritreans. And those who disparage the Mafia are already victims. In St. Vincent's case more money is swindled through our offshore banks from US accounts than our total annual budget!

Private agony multiplies into a public posture and in turn formulates foreign policy. The country that will help you shed your oppressor is your friend. Thus it is that internal frustration in Latin America breeds external support for civil strife. The ingredients of that cocktail now exist in the Caribbean. Then the United States plunges in, not when democratic principles are (first) negated, but in the climax of the confrontation when reasonable men have long perished. For it is always the strategy of the extreme left to destroy the Centre advocating reform so that oppression matures and international socialist solidarity can be upheld as the only avenue of salvation.

Democracy is a delicate young seedling in the Caribbean. Incipient authoritarianism threatens peace. Grenada today we must not forget is a product of cheated elections and the collapse of institutions under repression. It is the early signal attacks on democratic institutions that must be arrested. A sentence here or there in a law undermining free and fair elections does not seem to deserve anyone's attention until holy hell breaks loose. Guyana is the best example of legally perverse elections. St. Vincent has just established rigid control of the electoral process by the Executive, complete with clauses to undermine the secrecy of the ballot. Heaped on these abuses covert financing of wicked administrations simply postpones the retribution.

In the face of all the conflicts emerging out of our political systems, the US should be mindful of the real areas of linkage that exist between the US and the Caribbean. Hardly a tomato is grown except from seeds supplied by a US firm. The same goes for lettuce, cabbages and every vegetable. And agricultural diversification is the main prerequisite of our development. What fertile ground for American influence.

Had Britain through its Commonwealth Development Corporation not imposed 220 volts/50 cycles, every piece of electrical equipment would be imported from the US. Indeed the sooner we can streamline our industrial energy to US standards, the better.

Not a single tourist arrives in the Caribbean from Eastern Europe. Our agriculture, industry and tourism are linked to North America and Europe. Sooner or later, all unproductive adventurism into other areas will come home to roost. Some 4000 artists and writers from our area went to Cuba for Carifesta. None stayed. Had such a festival been held in New York, the authorities would still be searching for those specialising in criticism of US culture.

Every single family in the Caribbean has relatives in the US or Canada. For all these influences how can we not feel close to the US and Canada.

However, ill-considered foreign policy by the United States in particular can destroy the influence of all these natural economic influences. Tyranny, victimization, arbitrary use of official power creating a terrible living situation in the islands, if supported by the US will drive the population to emotional refuge elsewhere. The errors of policy that have created El Salvador stare at us in the Caribbean and Latin America today. Let me repeat, the advocates of change and reform are the natural allies of the US.

It is within the framework of guiding change that lie opportunities for profitable investment through careful planning.

Development is about people. It ought not to be simply defined in terms of architecture, traffic jams, and joint communiques. When I look at the castles on an island like Mustique, risingout of the exquisite development plans, and compare them with the food on the plates of the original inhabitants nearby, I wonder what does progress mean? Capital injection that returns us to the slave plantation constitutes the path of despair. Had there been the slightest instinct for fair play or decency, some measure of parallel progress would have been possible. Not slums and castles!

I offer the concept of Parallel Progress between the investor and those on whom effort is invested, as a fundamental objective in any planning criteria.

One real area where the developed countries of this hemisphere can help us is in the field of education. Perhaps the greatest difference between rich and poor countries of the world is the quality of education. And the quality of people's education affects seriously the quality of their lives. The higher fees for foreign students in the advanced countries is the saddest inequity imposed on poor countries in recent years. That you should impose this burden on our educational opportunity makes us all poorer. The foreign student of Canadian technology will tend to enhance Canadian exports to his country. And to deny us a glimpse of your standards of academic excellence enshrines chauvinism at home as a national objective and clothes our intellectuals with their unnecessary mantle of self-righteousness. Scholarships for study at all levels in academic and and technical institutions in the US, Canada and Mexico and Venezuela should be a cornerstone of the Caribbean Basin Initiative. They should be awarded by a process of searching at the local levels, not simply allocated to governments as a handout to the children of Ministers, their cronies or their friends.

In the battle for the minds of the future generation of leaders what a great opportunity for influence is lost by not providing the opportunity to study at your institutions. It is not a relevant argument against scholarships that the trained people do not return. Some do, and those that do have more influence than the numbers suggest. And in any event, if they join the migrant community their influence at home cannot be ignored. A good education lasts a life-time, or more, as parents influence their children, and investment in people is what development is all about. Investment in talent will in the long run yield better dividends than guns for the coast guard. The battle for the minds begins with the mind.

President Reagan has announced new aid for the Caribbean. How will this aid be dispensed? Will existing institutions be used or will a new expensive bureaucracy be created? Will this self-perpetuating Conference Industry simply produce more resolutions, more documents for libraries, more long-winded radio announcements?

Bilateral aid to the countries directly, using criteria clearly established with defined performance schedules and re-evaluation mechanisms, will be the optimum way to address the problem of aid dispensation. Care must be taken to identify the correct projects—those that will improve the lot of the poor. Very often aid only reaches the rich in poor countries. Evaluation should continue throughout the life of the project and continuity should be built in, irrespective of the government in power. Many Caribbean governments abandon projects started by their predecessors simply because of spite. Barbados abandoned a cement project but has to come back to it. I will give you an example in my constituency of the Grenadines. A study for an airport in Bequia was undertaken by British and Barbadian consulting firms along with the Caribbean Meteorological Institute and was completed in May, 1974 at a cost of $130,000. This followed the $600,000 Tourism Development Strategy in May, 1972 which also recommended an airport. When the government changed, the project was dropped although no other project could help the people of the island more. Similarly the airport built on the island of Canouan in 1974 has not yet been declared a port of entry, for similar reasons. In the meantime less feasible projects with less social benefit and creating more burdens on the tax base, get priority.

President Reagan hopes to stimulate more private investment in the region. Private investors will do well to be guided more by the experience of existing investors in the country rather than by flowery assurances by government ministers at banquets in Washington. Let them research the government's performance, for example; how long does it take to get project approval? Are letters to the Prime Minister answered? Is bribery expected?

We are pleased that the United States has come to recognise the need for a new Initiative in the Caribbean and has re-discovered the importance of these islands. I trust that the value attached to the Caribbean will be matched by the calibre of US diplomatic personnel assigned to the region. There is no substitute for intelligent understanding of the region's aspirations, and this could well prevent frequent spasms of diplomatic epilepsy.

I started this paper indicating how difficult it is for the United States and the Caribbean to find a common definition of the enemy. President Reagan has identified the enemy as a foreign force. In my view the enemies are already within our gates: rigged and unfair elections, bribery, corruption, poverty, overpopulation, constitutions that cheat large sections of the people, incompetence at the highest level, and the despair of the half-educated. Those who help us to destroy these enemies will be our friends.

LAND REFORM IN THE CARIBBEAN

*CADEC lecture at the University
of the West Indies, Trinidad*

August 29th, 1972

LAND REFORM IN THE CARIBBEAN

I would like to express my appreciation to CADEC for inviting me to address you on the important subject of Land Reform in the Caribbean. Your invitation to me, as the organisers of this course will recall, came very early in the life of my Government when the superfluity of doubting Thomases questioned the life of the Alliance Government in St. Vincent. Your confidence in me once more demonstrates the greatest strength of the Church throughout the centuries, that of faith, and your pursuit today of a course in agriculture demonstrates that you intend to develop your faith based on a sound understanding of the fundamental problems confronting our Caribbean today.

It is not only to avoid quibbling on words that we should begin by defining what we mean by land reform, but also to establish the principles at which we aim. Some of these principles are universal, and some of the detail will remain specific so as to be adapted to the peculiar circumstances of our village states. Land reform in my view must be related to both the sectional interests of development in our region, both agriculture and tourism. Such reform means redistribution of land, mainly in the distribution of large areas into small farms, and also the consolidation of mini-plots into small farms.

Let me emphasise at the outset that the goal of any policy in land reform should be related to productivity. Merely dismantling large estates and granting title of small parcels to the greatest number of voters can deliver results in the next election, destroy the economy, create unemployment, and guarantee reverses in subsequent elections. Between the two extremes lie the scope for organised planning, based on the need to stabilize the human resources of the country and integrate this with the market requirements of the region as a whole.

Let us develop further the idea of stabilising the human resources of the Caribbean. The rhetoric today declares terms like "Get the people involved", "Let us control our resources", "Get the people back to the land" and the clarion call for "Dignity" pervades every aspiration.

With regard to involvement, there are differing degrees of relevance as to whether or not, this is accomplished in any instance. First of all, the unemployed may be said to be involved in the large plantation when a job becomes available, be it a seasonal job, or a permanent job. The ordinary unskilled exercise is indeed a fundamental experience in involvement, but the question immediately arises as to what extent is that person involved in the happenings of the estate. His physical self may participate, but involvement is a word encompassing the whole being of man, in the religious context defined as body and soul. When the whole state of man participates in the utilisation of his energy, and his rational, emotional, physical and spiritual elements are participating in his work, then we have a happy individual genuinely involved in what is going on, genuinely expressing himself, feeling he is doing his thing.

When I speak of land reform therefore, my objective is not only to secure continuous productivity, but in creating farm units where the farmer himself leads a fulfilling life and comes into his own. The material component of this indulgence is that the farm unit be compatible with the farmer's needs and the society of other farmers among whom he belongs.

The establishment of middle-sized family-owned farms will produce a better rural community. Such an organised community can not only share plant protection or marketing services, but also their common social and cultural facilities. The organisation of the family in this way should commend itself to the Church.

Within a purely theoretical framework too, we should note, concerning production, that if the same output is guaranteed by a large number of small farmers as would be produced by one large farmer on the same area of land, there remains greater opportunity for strengthening the State's economy in the first case than in the second. A greater number of self sufficient people all have the same requirements, and increasing their purchasing power will mean more expenditure than consolidation of savings. Increased consumption stimulates the economy. Increased participation in the economy, and increased stability with more people having a meaningful stake in the economy stabilises the democratic process.

I do hope that you note my emphasis on production. I have no interest in a material distribution to accomodate the lazy. My preference is to create opportunities for initiative and hard work.

168

MARKET REQUIREMENTS

There are basically two kinds of markets for our agricultural produce in the Caribbean, that of the extensive crops such as sugar cane and bananas grown for export to the European market, and the intensive vegetable crops grown for the Caribbean market. The Agricultural Marketing Protocol of Carifta is supposed to accommodate the second, and the problems of the British Entry into the European Economic Community affects the first. These two problems are not unrelated to the questions of land reform in the Caribbean.

Our experience in St. Vincent is that vegetable production is a peasant exercise. I recall the initiation of the AMP when my Ministry of Agriculture organised meetings with farmers, and I myself went along to these meetings, describing what a carrot and a carrot seed look like. A few years ago we imported all our requirements: today we export over 40, 000 pounds a month. The yield of wealth per acre from carrots far exceeds the return from bananas. The loving care required in the production of tomatoes, peppers and other intensive vegetable crops cannot be readily mobilized within the framework of the plantation system. The marketing opportunities now being withdrawn or created indicates quite clearly the urgent need for land reform if large areas of our region are not to become desolate.

My comments here should not be restricted to mean that we need land reform to produce food only for the Caribbean. Being in one geographic area, we are subject to the same periods of drought, and the same periods of glut, and there are commodities other than sugar and bananas which the export market in Europe and elsewhere require. I refer to crops like avocados, mangoes and other exotic tropical fruit; and within the Caribbean itself, land reform in any of the member States will not produce the necessary guaranteed results unless there is rationalisation of regional production, and guaranteed markets somewhere.

There is a tendency even in the rhetoric of some apostles of development that we need industrialisation to reduce unemployment. While this may be so, many who make these bland statements, see industry as some high wage earning operation as distinct from agriculture. The best form of industrialisation is using local resources. Many opportunities await us in industrialisation based on produce from our farms.

Those who have the oil resources may find the capital to bring about the structural changes required in the agricultural sector. But the situation is very difficult for other less fortunate Caribbean States, with 50 per cent of the population under 16 years old, where capital formation may long remain a dream. Most lending agencies are prepared to help finance the development of farms, where title is already secure. Generally finance is not available to purchase the land. If cash is not available, the land will have to be purchased with trading the other unquestioned asset conferred on us by birth, and it is Time. In our situation in St. Vincent one per cent of the farmers own forty eight per cent of the arable land. We need not look at the unemployment of young people in the cities, and initiate propaganda programmes to get them back to the land, unless we make arrangments for them to own the land, and provide the credit, training and opportunity for them to lead fulfilling lives as farmers.

An effective land reform programme cannot be financed by the small islands themselves. Our land holding situation is a direct heritage from colonialism, and the colonial powers are aware of the need for fundamental improvements in their own land holding structure in their development programmes. In the European Economic Community, hundreds of millions of dollars are spent on these programmes each year. The Caribbean islands have a right to expect greater capital assistance for the implementation of any region wide long range land reform programme from former colonial powers. Let us not only talk of Economic Communities but the Community of mankind and our international interdependence.

THE INFLUENCE OF TOURISM

Now let me turn to the influence of tourism on agriculture. The first problem is the inflation of land prices. The problem of a dock strike in England may make the difference between the profit and loss for a farmer in a particular year and encourage him to dispose of his land. The high values on beach land are creeping into the countryside and the valleys twenty minutes from the beach. A capital sale of one acre of land may provide more income than the

170

farmer has known for many years. The farmer hardly stops to think that the cash in his hand loses its value daily and that when this cash is exhausted he is without a means of livelihood. There are sad cases where people have sold their resources, dreaming when they did so that they would have enough to see them to the end of their days. Then they wind up being on the wage list of the purchaser, who is speculating on the resources of the local people, without any foreign investment, making use of loans and mortgages from local banks.

Now above all, we need to strike a balance. We need to establish our objectives, we need to integrate our tourism with agriculture. We need both.

Firstly, it is necessary that we zone our country. This involves the use of all the technical expertise available, to classify the land in accordance with soil type, slope, crop utilisation and so on.

Secondly, we need to define the area for hotels and other tourist and industrial facilities. The overall plan will therefore show areas of forests, national parks, agriculture and tourism. Let us define the areas in which we relax, and the areas in which we sweat. Having established the pattern of usage in various zones, the zoning must be protected and enforced.

Above all we must destroy the myth that large plantations will one day be cut up into hotel sites, and create the fundamental framework for meaningful agriculture. A potentially high price for land, unrelated to agricultural productivity alienates the land from any immediate agricultural purpose.

Let me make passing reference to the need to reform certain attitudes in land development. The whole question of agrarian reform is not simply a material consideration related to the area of the earth's surface that produces a certain quantity of wealth, but a reorganisation of people in relation to the earth from which they came. Very often I have received development programmes spread out on enormous sheets of paper, beautifully designed in different colours, reserved green belts, residential zones, hotel sites, winding roads, shopping arcades, etc. The developers train their eye on the land, seek out the very stone on which the best Madison Avenue romantic advertisement may be dreamt, and they relate very appropriately the use of the land asset to the financial return. One may listen to a theme of this kind over several hours, and not a word is said about developing people. With more specific relevance, no attention is paid to the development of the people who belong to the land. Any genuine concept of land reform must begin with the fundamental metaphysical concept that recognises not merely the law of property, namely that the land belongs to people, but also that the people belong to the land. Our Christian heritage recognises this in the last rites conferred on our existence, in the theme "ashes to ashes, dust to dust". Let us have the same rights established during our existence and have a reasonable area of land relate to the man while he is sweating upon it. While so many investors panic in the continuing quest for security of investment, it is so because they ignore the need for security among others. Any investment that offers security, or protects the livelihood of some people will be protected by those people. In this context again, I will stress that selfishness does not sustain our democracy.

One of our greatest tourist attractions in a State such as St. Vincent is our agricultural activity. The tourist loves the beautiful scene of the different shades of green in our different crops, up and down the well contoured slopes. If this activity perishes, the tourist will find no beauty in the land and find the conversations with other tourists quite boring. The impact of tourism must be related to an agricultural land reform programme also, for it is important that any settled farm remains a farm as long as it is in the best interest of the country that it should be so.

This leads to the problems of establishing continuity where the changes through land reform have been organised. It brings us back to the criterion of productivity. In the beginning of the programme we may establish the criterion of an efficient unit, including the level of farm income related to labour supply and the commodity price available. These factors of evaluation may change, but continuity of production will only be maintained if the farm unit meets the sociological requirements of the farmer. Very critical in this is the avoidance of fragmentation through inheritance. This problem may be reduced by the establishing of the framework on which the land reform programme is based. Help the farmer to understand this and in turn he will subscribe to the values on which the continued success of the venture depends. This problem of the difficulty of avoiding fragmentation, points to the other essential sectors of

172

development that must take place elsewhere in an economy which must absorb some of the farmer's children.

All plans need adjustment, but above all there should be a central authority evaluating the process of any adjustment, so that the criterion of the country's productivity may be steadily analysed. The tools of continuity must be established in legislation that initiates the system, and also legislation that sustains its momentum.

One of the fundamental concepts of your Christian faith is: "Love thy neighbour as thyself". You know far better than I the universal religious definition of who constitutes one's neighbour. In a very real sense, when we look at a structural land reform programme, we may well say that the object of such a programme would be to get the farmers to love one another as themselves. For surely if they have equivalent status, growing the same crops, dependent on the same degree of rainfall, responsive to the incidence of the same pest and diseases, with adjoining farms of the same size, how will praedial larceny commence? Surely the real groundwork is there, binding these men in the same fate, sponsoring their real love of one another, their land and their country.

We come therfore to conclude that we need land reform in the Caribbean.

(1) Because an analysis of our land resource demonstrates the inequity in our heritage.

(2) The structural requirement in modernising our economy by distributing wealth and increasing consumption demands the change.

(3) Our free enterprise system requires more participants in the system if the system is to survive.

(4) The scarcity of our land resources demands its efficient and intensive use. Moreover, we cannot afford the under utilisation of valuable land that is practised in some areas.

Our demand that we control our resources cannot simply mean that Government must own everything and be the sole employer in the State. For me, ownership of the resources mean vesting title in the people so that they assume responsibility for production. Dignity will come through the expression of our energies in producing the foods for the sustenance of our well being. In speaking about a single subject such as this, one danger is that an over emphasis be given. Land reform at best, remains one instrument of change. There are others. Without a re-education in the Caribbean to redirect people's minds to the significance of our agricultural base in our lives, a new land utilisation programme may be no more than a distraction. We must analyse our problems, set them into perspective, have the courage to take decisions and bring about orderly change. How can we love our country if none of it is ours!

The accomplishment of these objectives in planning the development of our land and people will require a massive, integrated and well coordinated effort by all the institutions concerned, and if you accept what I have said, I call on you, CADEC, and the Church in the Caribbean to lend your support for this task.

TO HELL WITH PARADISE

*A New Concept in Caribbean Tourism
Address at the Caribbean Travel Association
Press Conference, Haiti*

TO HELL WITH PARADISE

Perhaps I should begin by making it easy for you to identify where I am from by reminding you that my country St. Vincent is the land where the Soufriere volcano erupted last year. Perhaps I may introduce myself in letting you know what sort of leadership St. Vincent now has by saying that I was the Minister who climbed the crater when the action started to test the temperature of the water. When everyone thought we were perishing we had the most exciting experience of our life watching the creation of the newest island in the world.

For the last five years I have been a Minister of Tourism. The important thing is not so much my experience, but the experience of all of us in the last five years of Caribbean Tourism. This period has been one of great success and of great gloom, both in terms of what was happening to the source of our dollars and the values that were on trial in the region.

I am satisfied that in January of this year Caribbean Travel Association brought together a formidable body of intellect to examine the problems of Caribbean Tourism and our market. A searching analysis does not always produce the appropriate solution, any more than meteorological equipment helps us avoid storms; still it provides us with an opportunity to know where we are going, where we ought to go if we are going, where we ought to go if we are pursuing certain objectives, and how to avoid a certain kind of elementary disaster. At this point in time, a very important separation has got to be made. On the one hand we have the problem of investment. That investment should remain tied to a hunt for profits. Name the system, however varied, the objective remains the same. On the other hand, we have the problem of people struggling to find a new way of life in an evvironment that has never yet yielded such a way of life.

Tourism is vacation business. But it is no vacation for the hotel manager or the maid, no matter how closely either of them may identify with this experience for a short transitory moment, it is not a vacation for either of them.

The real separation I want to make is between two types of people:

A: THE INVESTOR
B: THE TOURIST

These two are absolutely separate. It is true that many a tourist on a beautiful holiday decides, here is heaven. This is where I want to spend the rest of my days. Wouldn't it be wonderful if I can stay here, make a dollar and have a ball in the process.

The trouble, though in this process, is that the aspect changes. Many an investor in the Caribbean behaves as though he is on a holiday, and can't understand how it has come about that an area that once was receptive, has changed so fundamentally, and is hostile to him. The fact is, that the area has not changed. He, the tourist, has become investor. He does not know that in this world, each of us knows the difference between giving and receiving, that the tourist giving of himself and his savings, is not the same role for the investor hunting his profit.

Very often the investor who runs into trouble by asserting values that are hostile to the environment, and in his delusion and pique, would declare the environment hostile. He declares "The people don't like us anymore". And in his all embracing "us", he classifies tourist and investor in the same breath. Even though he may know the difference, it may suit his spirit of revenge, for his failure to assert his own values, and the hope of creating disharmony in tourism in the future.

In using tourism to improve the economy of the Caribbean, governments have made mistakes. In the effort to secure more than a lazy six percent on capital on fixed deposit, and using tourism to fulfil this goal, investors too have made mistakes. It is therefore wrong for politicians solely to blame foreign investors for the problems created by the investment lured to their country, even as it is pointless for investors to scream when the pendulum they have pushed swings against them. We must acknowledge our errors, and see how best we can exploit the fact that one of the greatest untapped resources for pleasure for the industrialised North American still lies in the Caribbean. The sins of the past need be exposed, and new approaches in the same environment need be created.

Perhaps one myth that needs to be exploded is the idea of the Caribbean Paradise. Let us face it, there is no paradise, only different ways of life. Not that Paradise has been lost, or destroyed but that it never existed, neither here nor in the Pacific. Each day, every living soul must face the problems of his own existence. The problems of New York or

Toronto may not be the problems in the Grenadines. The North American trying to escape a big city problem like air pollution may not recognise the West Indian's problem of lack of opportunity in a small island. But it is a problem just the same and a serious one.

In all this sea of confusion that exists in tourism, perhaps it is appropriate that I define our tourism model, that I give you an outline of our policy in St. Vincent. I make no assumption that ours is the correct approach; I recognise others are quite entitled to do their own thing, as we say. The tourism market constitutes several hundred million people, but we are not interested in appealing to 100 million people. We are a small country of many islands, including the Grenadines, with less than 1000 hotel rooms. We aspire to increase our hotel capacity at a pace that will grow steadily, not one that has a sudden burst of investment that shocks everybody, and creates sociological difficulties.

We want to attract the kind of people who are interested in what we have to offer. Our beaches are as good as any, our agricultural activity brighter than many other areas in the Caribbean. We have no casinos, million dollar complexes, or French cuisine. We specialise in small hotels where the manager gets to know the guest, and the ambience is local. We insist on good food, local cuisine with fresh home grown food and cleanliness in our hotels.

A number of people in the tourism business complain to Trade Ministers that they need a licence to import frozen vegetables, smoked salmon and the like, so as to serve the kind of menu the visitors want. My attitude is that we do not want the visitors who want pre-packaged mass produced food. We are a small and different place. We have a volcano that erupted in 1902 and last year, and we like our volcano, our local vegetables, our life style, and we invite you the visitor to come and share the things we like. If you want smoked salmon, go to British Columbia where I know they have the best salmon in the world. If you want fresh lobsters and king fish, come our way. When as a visitor, you support our fishing industry by demanding our fish dishes, then you are stimulating the development of our own indigenous activity which in turn makes our country interesting for you.

The integration of tourism with other sectors of the economy, be it in production of local exotic dishes or in the manufacture of local furniture for small indigenous hotels creates a genuine involvement of our people, and gives them a stake in the tourist industry which they will want to protect. Indeed what greater fun can there be for the visitor who loves fishing to spend a day with men who are fishing for their living! When you enjoy our singing and purchase our art and crafts, you are stimulating the development of our people in a way that makes us ever more interesting.

The tourist who comes to our country loves to drive through our countryside. This appreciation of the countryside has got to be tied in with the menus in the hotels if the farmer is going to find markets for his product and we as a country are going to retain an increasing share of that tourist dollar.

However our land capability planning has got to demonstrate a zoning of tourist and agricultural activity and the land reserved for hotels carefully differentiated from agriculture, otherwise the inflation of land values in tourism may force the land out of farming.

We seek therefore an integrated tourism, one in which various sectional interest in our economy are all accommodated.

One of the great things about the CTA poster for this meeting, printed by Andre Normil, is the vitality of Haitian life demonstrated, in which the tourist is participating. You get the feeling that the visitor while enjoying himself has become part of the action while he is there, but that the action will be proceeding without him. The visitor is therefore not imposed on the local community. He is a guest. A great deal of conflict is avoided if we recognise this and seek to develop this pattern. This kind of experience, as for example; sailing on the local schooner with the cases of beverages and cartons of vegetables, adds local colour to the visitors experience. The tourist indulges an acute sense of place. This cultural sense of place, which appeals to people seeking new experience, and looking forward to knowing more about themselves, and the world, is what we have to offer. That is why those who discover our country return so often. That is why so many visitors seek retirement homes in our community. And so those who were once visitors become hosts, participating in developing the special sense that ours is a different place.

Now when you visit a country, enjoy it and want to return to live there, there should be no sense in wanting an alien architecture and wanting to change the environment. It is not that we consider our living situation perfect, it is simply that we should keep what we have that is good and you the visitor or investor should seek a way to blend what we have to offer with your needs. No purpose either for yourself or for us will be served by your wanting what we cannot offer and feel that we are depriving you, when it was your choice to come to us and our choice to invite you to accept and pay for what we offer. It makes nosense wanting to build a lavish New York home in the Caribbean with gold plated faucets and the like. Build with our materials, use the methods we have tested; be very careful that your improvements are genuine improvements and those that blend with our environment. We want an indigenous tourism of high value, not the incompatible mass product!

We do not need the development of any Miami Beach along any of the 22 miles of white sand beaches in our country. We want the kind of investment. the kind of attitude that will be of permanent value to our people and of permanent interest to our visitors. This way the investment is safe and tourism is permanent. Nothing that I say contradicts the images of sun and sea and sex that the advertisement sponsors. It is just that beyond this we like to feel we provide a special kind of ambience in which these indulgences are part of it all. This interesting way, in our view, invites people to stay with us longer, and learn to enjoy the place.

Throughout the Caribbean today as in many parts of the world there is growing concern about control of our resources. To me this does not mean we become more insular than we are, that we become more chauvinistic, and abandon the mainstream of development in the rest of the world. Under capitalised as we are, we still need foreign expertise, guidance, cash and help. Again I must stress, we must separate the visitors from the investors. Our own people have only enough money for small hotels under thirty rooms. With this status hotel we are quite pleased. For us the best form of foreign investment is that of partnership with local people. This means we have the best of two worlds; that both the local investor and foreign investor have an interest in the development of our country and people on the one hand and the healthy development of our market overseas on the other. I would encourage foreign investors to seek suitable local partners. We operate a system of free enterprise; we are as committed to it as you are, and we must seek ways to create meaningful relationships.

In this way too we are looking at ways and means of getting visitors into local homes, and getting twinning programmes with sister cities so that we extend the human contact at all levels of our tourism.

At home, our political programme is one of seeking unification with our neighbours. Accordingly, Grenada, St. Lucia and St. Vincent have recently taken an important decision to permit freedom of movement to our people and out visitors within their States. We hope soon to extend this first step at unifying our people to include our sister islands. We are busily looking outward to enhance all that we already inwardly possess.

As Premier of my State, you will pardon me I hope if I appear not too anxious to grab the easiest dollar. I have said in our brochure on St. Vincent and the Grenadines that in tourism our aim is the development of our people while giving our guests good value. The tourist dollar alone, unrestricted is not worth the devastation of my own people. I want to attract the kind of investor and the kind of visitor who would understand this and need this kind of climate. A country where the people have lost their soul is no longer a country—and not worth visiting.

I know that it is difficult to ask the ad men to remove that word Paradise from their vocabulary. But I know that there is a market of people who want to get away from man made perfection, whose idea of a holiday is not heaven, but participation in a different experience. Our islands, our villages, our small hotels can offer this. And there is a beautiful reciprocity in our relationship with this type of tourist, for as much as we are able to appeal to him, he in turn with his real interest in our way of life is the most likely to appeal to us.

So this is our model. Those who are satisfied with the way they are going please excuse me if we are different. Pardon me then if I am sacrilegious in saying: to hell with paradise. After all this is life.

THE CARIBBEAN MINI STATE; THE EXQUISITE ISLES

Extract from an address to the
World Affairs Council of
Northern California
San Fransisco

November 21st, 1973

THE CARIBBEAN MINI STATE;
THE EXQUISITE ISLE

I have attempted to evaluate the material components of life in the Associated States. I have not elaborated on our social problems, nor have I outlined how we are stimulating and diversifying our agriculture in an attempt to feed ourselves. Indeed St. Vincent produces more local food than any other of the Associated States. Nevertheless the trade statistics have shown our reliance on the rest of the world. We too are victims of inflation, with our sensitive bread prices responding to the world-wide grain shortage, with our fish prices responding to oil prices which are responding to the Arab-Israeli conflict.

We are therefore a bunch of small islands sensitive to the pressures of inflation bedeviling life elsewhere. Small islands so reliant on imported materials for shelter and sustenance, pay an expensive price for survival. Increasing unemployment accompanies our inflation, and with 50% of our population under 16, the solution is not around the corner. But we have to find answers, including special oil prices for the Third World.

The problem of increasing deficits is not only a problem of the Associated States. No big thing you'll say, as developed countries like the United States live with it all the time. But the parameters for a mighty country and ours are not the same. For us it is the story of life and death. The independent Caribbean countries face the same problem. Their independence has hardly protected them from what remains essentially the geography of the Caribbean. The rest of the world sees the Caribbean basin as one region, and the Caribbean needs to greet the rest of the world with one voice if we are to exert any influence on the international forces controlling our destiny. As far as I am concerned there is no need to increase the number of independent strident voices, increasing the cacophony.

Only on a very large map of the world is the shape of Jamaica indicated, and Jamaica is the largest of the Caribbean islands. Seldom do the number of dots include all the Caribbean islands with resident populations. The tragedy is that the residents on these small islands have not grasped the significance (or the insignificance) of their size, and among others things demand insular solutions to problems like inflation, totally oblivious to the world market forces, and the insignificant role in trade reciprocity that a market of 100,000 people can play. Protected by the cloak of our chauvinism some of us seriously feel that the rest of the world knows or cares about the difference between Anguilla and Antigua, or between Grenada and Tobago.

The need for a strong central government in the Associated States cries out from every problem, every source of conflict, whether it be in the fixing the price of eggs or fixing airfares with international carriers, maintaining a respectable Judiciary vital to the security of the fundamental rights in the Constitution, locating industries to relieve unemployment, or securing the right talent within the framework of economies of scale that will begin to produce a modicum of perfection, be it in medicine or administration. It is difficult to determine standards even when the choice is wide; imagine how indifferent the standards and how self defeating the exercise when the comparison is narrow.

The kindness of our climate is an enemy of change, for it produced no challenges. Our heritage of slavery can be blamed for our hostility to manual work. The imperialists can be blamed for the failure of the West Indies Federation. Guyana can be blamed for stimulating the Grenada Declaration* and Trinidad can be blamed for staying out. The investors can be blamed for the paucity of local chefs in our restaurants. And so the convenient excuses are perpetuated.

In fact, there are neither pat excuses nor pat answers. One has got to be realistic, and at the same time imaginative. Isolationism for the Caribbean as a whole is ridiculous and for States within the Caribbean to pursue institutional insularity as as a way of life is even more senseless. We must sell our primary commodities. For bananas and sugar that means association with the European Economic Community. In turn, this exercise has brought us to seek common cause with Africa and the Pacific region also seeking trade expansion with Europe. Closer to home, we have exchanged greetings with Venzuela, but it is too early to tell what will come of this. After an appropriate grace, one awaits the hors d'ouevre with relish. The point is, small as we are, we must look outward.

To look out, we must first look in, and about ourselves. If there is to be any broad determination of purpose in the Caribbean as a whole, there needs to be a certain equality among the States thus grouped. It is hard to see how this can be accomplished, without first a coming together of the minute Associated States with a single political voice presenting theirs as a single view in and beyond the region. Herein lies the real prospect of our survival. How long will it take for the clarity of this view to demand the responses to convert this into reality, before it is too late!

For make no mistake about it, the denial of reason, the loss of a sense of beauty or the right of personal choice, and the collapse of our fundamental freedoms may well take our indifference and complacency by surprise if we fail to act.

Mini-States, like minatures, are for collectors. Exquisite, dead!

*The declaration was issued in Grenada calling for a new union in the Caribbean.

ENVIRONMENTAL CONFLICT IN ISLAND STATES

Paper presented at the
Fourth Grafton Conference
on Economic Development
Grafton, Vermont

June 9th, 1985

ENVIRONMENTAL CONFLICT IN ISLAND STATES

A friend of mine, a passionate lover of the islands in the Caribbean once said to me:

"Son, these islands were not meant to be inhabited."

When one thinks about the inadequacy of flat lands for playing fields in a small island, the impossibility of getting away from noise pollution, denudation of beaches by the removal of the limited quantities of sand to build houses, and the destruction of an island environment in a lifetime, such a sentiment seems to be not without merit.

But in spite of it all, my eyes do not tire of the beauty of the small islands in the Grenadines where I was born. To sit in the shade of a tree and witness a sunrise looking across the blue Caribbean towards other islands in the distance, to listen to the mountain doves, and pigeons cooing, and the mocking birds mimicking away, even as a yacht goes sailing by, a yacht that has perhaps even travelled a thousand miles to be part of this scene: all this compensates and signals another sentiment, that the world still has its own beauty and we should never tire in planning to keep it that way.

In contemplation of the good of an environment, we begin with evaluating a sense of beauty. At the other extreme, we become pained by the destruction of the environment, particularly when this destruction of the ecology by man leads to his own starvation and death. The holocaust in Ethopia and the lands perishing under the invading Sahel in Africa tell a gruesome message of man's failure to nurture his environment. Contrast this situation with the continuing capture of the desert by Israeli technology and we recognise that the environment can be made to bloom, that we can win the battle if we have the will to do it, and leave our corner of the world a better place for succeeding generations if we make this an ambition.

Now, no one in their right sense would cut down the breadfruit tree, as we say at home, from which he gets his sustenance. When forests are destroyed to produce firewood, the peasant who does this does not know, and does not believe that this would one day make him or his children thirsty. The fisherman who sells female lobsters with thousands of eggs, while he knows it is against the law, does not think the law is enacted to preserve his interests: he simply is studying his immediate requirements, and leaves it up to God and his elected representatives to provide for the future.

In my youth, all over the Caribbean you could find a lobster suitable for cooking close to the shore. This seems to be an experience which no other generation, for all time, will ever know.

The tragedy is simply one of population pressure on the scarce resource of the island community. It is in this sense that my cynical friend was right when he said "These islands were not meant to be inhabited".

So the land mismanaged becomes inhospitable. Man makes his fellowman first into an immigrant, and then into a refugee and the immigrants seek a greener pasture where others have learnt to make their environment productive.

The drought in Africa, caused by abuse of the land, and acid rain in North America and Europe are end products of mismanagement of our resources. We have to recognise the context of time, the vast scale of which our period of life is but a short and critical part. Nature unfolds its blessings within the context of millions of years, yet insensitive use of a resource created over such an extensive period can be destroyed in a lifetime. Many have ruined the vast jungles of Brazil and Africa in the attempt to convert them into great farms, only to realise that instead they have created a desert. What looks like lush tropical rainforest is no more than a beautiful forest cover evolved over the centuries as a delicate balance between the trees, the soil, and the atmosphere: The cycle is a harmony based on organic humus, and this is quickly converted into a wasteland when disturbed.

The evolution of an environment in this sense of time can be no better described than in the classical hymn:

"A thousand ages in Thy sight
are like an evening gone. . . "

We who are limited to our own experience of time need to learn the value of timelessness in which our environment was created. We should not in the short time span we are allocated, ruin the environment that Nature has taken millions of years to produce. The least we can do is leave it as we found it.

In our island societies in the Caribbean, economic management of the environment does not pose the problems of exremes as obtain in certain parts of the world. Our equitable climate almost by definition keeps us away from the extremes of flood and drought, but the scale of natural disaster far exceeds that on a continental land mass. The path of a hurricane through the Caribbean to North America may only destroy a section of Florida, but will disrupt the total economy of the island state in some cases almost irretrievably. Similar social dislocation can be effected by a volcanic eruption. The problem is one of size and scale. The island is always so vulnerable.

OVER POPULATION:

Fundamentally, the real problem of economic management of the environment in poor countries is the stress caused by over-population on the land. With population doubling every twenty-five years, how does one cope with the quantity (let alone quality) of housing, upgrading of transport systems, water and power delivery, education and health services, when one begins with limited resources? On top of all these natural restrictions, the isolated island community discovers new appetites through entertainment by satellite television and which the immediate resources cannot accommodate. So that planning environmental use today in the remotest island has to come to terms with an extraordinary imbalance of demands, and some of them totally unrelated to essential local needs.

The structure in most volcanic islands in the Caribbean is simply one of a mountain ridge in the centre, with deep valleys and a varied coastline. The habitable proportion of land varies, but by and large, the central ridge of mountains is inhospitable and should be preserved as forest cover to protect the water resources.

In almost every case there is legislation on water resources protection and this is adhered to in varying degrees.

The first problem of water resources and forest management is political. The landless, ill-educated and unemployed person cannot willingly understand that he should not denude the forest to earn his livelihood. As far as he is concerned, rain has always come in the rainy season. He is a man without tradition, no knowledge of records, no concept whatsoever about drought in Africa except that the transistor radio announces that famine is a subject that creates spontaneous relief effort. The real difficulty is how to communicate to this person, how to find him an alternate means of livelihood, how to convert him into a protector of the environment.

Legislation provides the first formal step, but laws cannot

protect a community from itself. In some cases, the political leadership is without the will to lead a community, and the community leads in the fashion of its own self-preservation, hoping that there are other answers to the removal of the forest cover. People in certain uneducated communities are capable of destroying the forest cover and still think that divine Providence will produce rain.

There is no greater visible tragedy in the Caribbean of the loss of forest cover than in Haiti. This Creole nation shares an island with the Spaniards in the Dominican Republic, and both lands have inherited the same geography. As you fly over them you can almost define their boundaries from the air. Haiti is bare, and the Dominican Republic is forested. The Haitian dictatorship considers the bare earth a permanent security measure against revolution, and poverty itself has hacked away at the environment. Soil erosion is phenomenal. I will venture to say that certain parts of Haiti, ruined in the last thirty years, are permanently irredeemable, and the tragic destruction of the environment will remain the nation's most cruel historical record. I say this not to mitigate the social evils of the dictatorship, but to emphasise that while tyrants will always perish, when they ruin the environment, they leave behind a permanent tragedy beyond correction by any new management.

Scorched earth policies have been well known tools of war, but using soil erosion as a security mechanism for peace and so called stability is the meanest form of leadership.

POLLUTION:

Let me now deal with the more normal problem of mismanagement, that of pollution, as we face it in the islands.

Our communities everywhere may well be classified in the way we deal with garbage, and indeed what constitutes the garbage. When the countryside is littered with disused containers it speaks volumes about the people who belong there.

As a young man hitchhiking through Europe when hitchhikers were adventurers and not parasites, I lived simply on bread, milk, sausages, fruit and wine. In Switzerland I could not avoid the chocolates. While the word exotic usually conjures up extravagant scenery in the tropics, for me the discovery of Swiss chocolates in Switzerland was really an indulgence in exotic tastes.

I dropped a wrapper on a sidewalk in Geneva. Soon an

old lady was tapping on my shoulder: "You dropped this," she said, returning my wrapper, "In Switzerland, we have a place for this", and she pointed to the baskets provided. I thanked her and apologised. I am still thanking that inspired lady in Switzerland, and today I find myself having to apologise for the garbage in our beloved islands.

Garbage disposal is one of the most horrendous problems in a small island. Where do you put it out of sight? If there is a swamp, sanitary fill is the answer. But when the single swamp is filled, what next? Do you import expensive technology which you cannot maintain? Will you let refuse produce an eyesore on the land or will you dump it in the ocean beside you. The answers are not simple, and drive planning authorities to distraction.

Luxurious yachts on principles learnt elsewhere will not dump their refuse in the deep ocean but will bring it ashore to a small island, sometimes one not much larger than the yacht itself.

Very often the disposal of garbage is not disposal at all. One individual gets rid of his problem, and in so doing creates a problem for someone else. We all want to get rid of our garbage, we don't want it around us, but do we care what becomes of it when dumped in another neighbourhood.

There seems to be a great universality in the garbage problem. The America one sees between the Kennedy airport and the United Nations Headquarters in Manhattan seems to tell us that even rich communities cannot bring basic pollution under control.

No system within an administration seems more capable of breaking down than garbage disposal. People who impose the most severe standards on themselves are quite capable of other attitudes when away from their own ambience. It is as though we have not learnt the international interpretation of the message from Mt. Sinai, "love thy neighbour as thyself", and that we have a duty to help to make not only our bedrooms beautiful but every place that we happen to be. Indeed the lady with the wrapper in Switzerland was so right: Why did a West Indian want to pollute Switzerland!

Economies that are not self-reliant must depend heavily on imports. Choice of the quality of container in such circumstances is restricted, and cannot be limited to disposable wrappers. When we talk of world trade, and the movement of goods in relation to the movement of payments, we seldom relate this to the problem of environmental pollution. Is

France or California concerned about the fate of empty wine bottles, or Scotland worried about the bottles without scotch, or the Japanese about wrecked cars littering the world's countryside? Some of our most beautiful beaches are ruined by wine bottles and plastic containers of Evian Water, from France left over from many a good party.

On the other hand, what we export from the Caribbean and Latin America, is usually biodegradable. Coffee, cocoa, bananas, nutmegs all vanish, so that in a very simple sense there is a real imbalance in trade between industrial and developing countries, one exporting well marketed containers that litter the landscape, the other exporting biodegradable commodities.

I do not apportion blame for this imbalance, as each of us choose what we want to import. But perhaps it is appropriate that I plead for a little forbearance. When you travel to the tropics and feel a little disgusted with the refuse in the developing countries, remember it may have been exported there from your country!

I do not however set this forward as an apology for our untidiness, or a rationalisation for our poverty.

ARCHITECTURE OF THE POOR:

Is there such a thing as architecture of the poor?

Modern cities can be refashioned out of vast resources, abundant wealth, and a pool of talent that can exercise unlimited choice. The poor island community, at its wits end to devise techniques of survival, has little flexibility in architecture.

But in spite of all the constraints, one can still ensure efficient use of materials and plan the landscape to produce pleasing results. I have found that over the years, the ambience of the community depends on the elbow room given around each house. As you plan a housing development for low incomes, the worse mistake is to restrict the size of plot. Nothing looks worse than lines and lines of identical huts with little vegetation. Diversity will always come from the gardens, for neighbours seldom plant the same flowers.

The question is, in the critical stage of planning a housing development for the poor, do the planners see the community escaping from poverty, do they expect the environment to develop, or are they planning an area of the earth surface to be a permanent slum.

I find it always a fascinating experience working on the financing of housing projects or subdividing lands to farmers, and watching how the financial unit called the house is transformed into the unit called home, and to see how a piece of land is transformed into the family farm.

There is a transitional point between expenditure of cash and creating the human environment.

I am satisfied that poverty need not be synonymous with ugliness, and that a sense of beauty and harmony in the environment can be served through simplicity. Indeed, the more limited the choice imposed by financial constraints, the more thought should be put into design.

The home is the permanent agent of continuity. Estate agents and developers sometimes do not look beyond the preoccupations of the market place, and do not recognise the responsibility to create an environment for living with any sense of continuity. Home is that place to which the person always wants to return; a house that is a resting place, the shelter that stimulates the occupant to play his role in his community.

THE MARINE ENVIRONMENT:

As though we in island communities do not have enough problems managing the environment of the land, we also have to pay attention to the marine zones around us.

St. Vincent and the Grenadines is a plural country, one main island with most of the population; and the archipelagic chain of Grenadine islands, some of them hardly more than a sand shoal, and others occupied by a resident population.

The islands are a haven for yachtsmen cruising the world, whether on the way from the Mediterranean to Panama, or from the South Atlantic to Fort Lauderdale. The remote islands then must support both fishermen and the international transients.

The scenery is idyllic, small islands surrounded by reefs constantly refreshed by the wide Atlantic, with gentle anchorages in which to rest from turbulent channels. But how does one protect these beautiful havens from human pressure, overfishing the seabed, trampling the plants, polluting the beaches?

The truth is that these areas cannot protect themselves, they need rigid rules and strict enforcement, or their beauty will vanish before our eyes and in our lifetime.

Modern fishing methods used by an ever increasing number of fishermen produced in the population explosion mean added pressure on the marine resources all the time.

On a more horrendous note, one real problem threatening the Caribbean is the possibility of oil spill from the supertankers constantly passing between the islands en route to the United States. This fact of our existence adds to our strategic value to the United States, but also creates one of our nightmares. One such spill can wipe out the tourist income in an island for a year, and create havoc in the environment for an inestimable period.

Some of our island communities have no economy outside fishing and tourism, so we are exceedingly vulnerable to the dangers of an oil spill. There are plans to deal with it, but they have not yet been tested.

CONCLUDING REMARKS:

I have emphasised the problems and the conflicts burdening the island community and have probably given the impression that our environment has been irretrievably ruined.

This certainly is not the case. But I prefer to draw attention to the problems. In your sophisticated rural communities in the United States, you can as in Vermont spend a fortune to restore your ancient buildings and monuments. It is marvelous to find opportunities to restore things. We in the Caribbean are not so fortunate. Our ancestors did not leave behind much architecture fit to be preserved from the last century. In those Colonial days our wealth in the Caribbean was used to build European cities. Ours is thus not a battle to restore or preserve the grandeur of a bygone age but to start now to build. We hope we can do so wisely.

BALANCING ECONOMIC DEVELOPMENT WITH ENVIRONMENTAL PROTECTION

Address on Conservation of the Americas,
Leadership Forum for the National Year of
the Americas, IUPUI, Indianapolis, Indiana

November 18-20th, 1987

BALANCING ECONOMIC DEVELOPMENT WITH ENVIRONMENTAL PROTECTION

In the last two decades, in the period since the Stockholm conference in 1972, the political will in the industrialised world has caught up with the language of the environmentalists. A more generalised international concern has recently matured in the present round of speeches in the General Assembly of the United Nations, and this new vital concern emanates from the work done under the auspices of Resolution 38/161 — the Brundtland Commission.

Within the framework of this international scenario, the first point I wish to make is the pressing need still to convey the knowledge of the importance of environmental protection, by and large understood in the developed world, to the communities in third world countries, the Caribbean being one. The urgency of the need to get that message across is intensified by the rate of technological transfer to these countries, for even as the new tools of exploitation like the power saw and the diving tank become more universally available, the greater becomes the rate of unfettered promiscuous degradation of both the forest and the sea bed.

I agree entirely with one of the simple answers arising out of the exhaustive intellectual analysis of the environment coming out of the Brundtland report; and I quote "Poverty is the major source of environmental degradation." To this I will add ignorance.

But one must temper this assertion with compassion. The charcoal burner, spurred on to make a better living both by his newly acquired power saw and the international energy crisis, (where some of the guilt lies) will not allow himself to care about the water resources of the next generation. He is not concerned about the millions of years of age of the forest cover in a small island mountain range, he is concerned only about the immediate income of his family. The lobster diver in the Caribbean still, unfortunately, does not care about selling female lobsters with millions of eggs as long as there are unscrupulous hotel owners willing to buy them.

But there is more insensitive abuse; the squatter who invades the land above the drinking water catchments, cultivating crops and using poisonous herbicides to enhance his yield, and in this process infects the environment with chemicals that last in the soil long after he himself is dead.

It goes without saying that it calls for harsh political

decisions to create a climate of opinion that allows common sense to prevail. In this audience of environmentalists, what you would assume to be common sense is plain heresy among the delinquent. It is common sense to know that if you eat all the eggs of a turtle you are reducing the catch of turtle meat, and yet, enforcing protection can be politically dangerous. The message of sustainable economic development, even for the egg poacher, takes longer than an election campaign. In some third world countries the level of political sophistication does not measure up to that which is needed to inaugurate an appropriate policy of environmental appreciation, but while we in the Caribbean are guilty of some insensitivity, I do not think we are beyond redemption. What is needed is the political will to press home the alternatives to environmental degradation while alternate avenues of economic activity are established.

I would summarise the specific environmental problems in our region as follows:

1. The use and abuse of non-biodegradable products such as plastics.
2. The destruction of forests for agriculture and charcoal production.
3. Uncontrolled attack on wildlife including foraging for eggs.
4. Removal of sand from beaches for the construction industry.
5. Pollution of reefs.
6. Overfishing of lobsters, turtles; particularly in the interruption of the reproductive cycles.

In addressing these concerns we, the policy makers, have to fit these problems into the macro-economic framework of our planning and decision making. Legislation with even stiff penalties can at best only produce intermittent control. In a democracy the least common denominator has a way of dominating social values among the uneducated, and we are in danger of having environmental abuse accepted as the norm. There is no way that one can legislate against bad government and one that translates the destruction of the environment into an assertion of the public will.

The last thirty years have seen more environmental degradation in the Caribbean than millions of years previously. I have seen in my lifetime entire colonies of birds, fish, and lobster vanish from what were once zones of abundance. The tragedy is that many assume this to be a natural progression.

Dealing with these problems, which are the end product of new technology and population expansion (as the new technology provides more efficient tools for a greater number of people to put more pressure on the limited resources), calls for careful thought and planning.

The same answers which deal with human population controls are relevant. First and foremost, proper education must be in place; and secondly, economic opportunity has to be provided. The person who will sell endangered species of parrot or a female lobster with eggs, like the drug dealer, genuinely believes that he has a right to earn his living by that means. Those of us who have learned other values can never relent in our efforts to demonstrate another path to progress.

Education hardly makes any impact on the way of thinking of the older generation. They have to be addressed with legislative sanction. I see more hope in educating the young.

You will excuse me if in addressing the economic opportunities that are necessary to create the climate for adequate environmental protection I refer to American foreign policy and its impact on development in Central America and the Caribbean. This is not the forum to go into any length into US trade and aid policies, but the issue is certainly relevant.

I want to draw your attention to the relevance, as I see it, to President Reagan's Caribbean Basin Initiative, its pending revision in the US Congress, and its impact on environmental protection in one part of the Americas. If the amendments to the Caribbean Basin Economic Recovery Act as now proposed become a reality, economic alternatives of gainful employment will be in place that will help us, the policy makers in the Caribbean, to provide what I would call environmental reform. And we would need to draw on the experience of international organisations to help us to create in our societies the consciousness that is fundamentally necessary. Our small societies in islands with populations under 100,000 cannot in any way threaten employment in the US.

Those of you who pride yourselves in being in the forefront of environmental protection in the US must take a little time to recognise that protectionism in the US also threatens environmental protection in poor countries!

The scale of operations in the Caribbean, especially in small nations with populations of 100, 000 people, can hardly put Americans out of work or create more degradation of your cities. A little scope in the US market will go a long way in providing economic development in the Caribbean. Alternate employment opportunities will ease the strain on the slender natural resources and enhance the legislative opportunity of the policy makers in dealing with environmental pollution and degradation.

I will end my presentation to bring to your attention what we have been doing in the last year in my country, St. Vincent and the Grenadines.

We enacted new modern and more effective legislation on the protection of birds and wildlife. Also new fisheries legislation, and regulations are in force, providing specific areas of environmental protection in what is call the "conservation zone".

Finally, the most beautiful area of land and sea in the East Caribbean, the mecca of the world's yachtsmen coming from the Mediterranean, the South and North Atlantic, and the area called our "Tobago Cays" are being acquired and established as a Maritime Park. We are about to inaugurate a foundation to be call "Friends of the Tobago Cays" and I will be happy to invite international participation in preserving this most beautiful spot in the Americas.

As we plan the 500th anniversary of the discovery of Columbus, it is fitting that between now and 1992 that we create among all our people a new consciousness of what our countries were like when Columbus came. The theme, if properly addressed to our young people, would inspire new attitudes for all time.

When one hears of the pollution of the Ganges, the horrendous impact of desertification in Africa, and the urban challenges in Bangladesh, one get a sense of despair. These catastrophes dwarf our problems in the Caribbean. But as though we need to learn the lessons of the universality of these problems, desertification in West Africa often now creates poor visibility in the Caribbean with the red dust we call "Sahara Haze", and this is an increasingly frequent phenomenon. You can imagine what will happen to our tourism industry if the blue Caribbean sky one day becomes only a memory.

In the Caribbean though, while we are a little late in coming to grips with our environmental problems—thank heavens we are not too late.

THE ROLE OF THE WORLD BANK AND THE INTERNATIONAL MONETARY FUND

Statement at the Commonwealth
Finance Ministers Meeting
St. Lucia

September 1986

THE ROLE OF THE WORLD BANK AND THE INTERNATIONAL MONETARY FUND

Mr. Chairman, much has already been said on the current world economic situation and prospects for growth in the industralised and developing countries. I do not propose to retrace that path, but it would be remiss of me if I were not to register my deep concern over the decline in total net flows of financial resources to the developing world, of which St. Vincent and the Grenadines and the East Caribbean are a part.

Preliminary estimates indicate that these flows declined from US $83 billion in 1984 to US $80 billion in 1985, the fourth successive annual decline since 1982.

Of equally great concern is the decline in net official development assistance received from the industrialised Commonwealth countries by the rest of the Commonwealth in 1985 over that received in 1984.

As we are all aware, prospects for growth of official development assistance for the rest of the decade are not more encouraging, given that this is estimated at a mere 2% per annum.

More specifically, we have witnessed marginal increases in gross World Bank Group disbursements from $11.1 billion in 1984 to $11.5 billion in 1985, as well as a decline in disbursements under the Fund's Standby and Extended Fund Facilities from SDR's $9.2 billion in 1983 to SDR's $3.0 billion in 1985. Borrowings under the Compensatory Financing Facility have declined over the 1983—1985 period as well. And all this, I might add, at a time when the world economic recovery remains fragile and uneven.

The above scenario becomes even more complex when one has got to grapple with the special problems which characterise small island states like my own. I refer here not only to our vulnerability to external economic shocks because of our degree of openness, but also to our poor resilience in the face of natural disasters because of our over-reliance on export agriculture.

Mr. Chairman permit me to draw on a recent experience to illustrate this point. On September 8th, 1986 tropical storm Danielle, swept over St. Vincent and the Grenadines for a period of three hours with winds of up to 45 miles per hour and gust up to 60 miles per hour. While there was no loss of life (and I thank God for that), in the aftermath of Danielle we ascertained that some 40% of our banana cultivation, our single most important foreign exchange earner, had been devastasted. That implies that there will be a net loss in foreign exchange to the country of some $15 million. In addition, significant damage was done to other crops and to property as well.

Two weeks after the storm, this very Monday, in fact when our soils were still saturated with water, a tropical deluge, inundating us with several inches of rain in a few hours, has caused severe damage, estimated at US $2.5 million to roads and houses. We have thus lost in a flash, all the gains we have made resulting from what can only be described as commendable management of our economy. In four hours of storms we can lose two percent of our GDP growth!

We in the smaller island states of the Caribbean are conscious of the need to diversify our economic base, not only within sectors but between sectors. We are also very aware that we face special problems related to economies of scale and agglomeration, problems of access to markets, problems of higher transport cost owing to our being some distance from the nearest market of any reasonable size, and problems of real income disparities.

We are fully aware that, as has been proven in so many other countries, embarking on any serious programme of economic adjustment with the objective of achieving sustainable growth and stability is a particularly painful process.

At the national level, our governments recognise that our management programmes already in place to improve our financial position, must continue, but in addition to all this we must have continuing access to resources on reasonable terms and conditions, to effect these changes in our economies.

Mr. Chairman, permit me again to draw on my country's experience. We in St. Vincent and the Grenadines, without a structural adjustment programme from the IMF, have had the courage to put in place a number of demand management controls much along the lines which the fund would have advised: all this not without cost to my people. We are now at a stage where we ought to strive to put in place growth oriented development programmes to expand our economy while emphasising our development priorities.

Let me say here, that while it has not been formally stated, we have already been told unofficially that the surest way to secure a sector adjustment loan with the Bank is to undergo a programme with the Fund! It looks, Mr. Chairman, as though carrying out the injunction from St. Paul, when he said: "For if Gentiles which have not the law, do by nature the things in the law, these having not the law, are a law unto themselves" is not appreciated. The move to link borrowing from one institution with borrowing from the other is to my mind a serious development, and while we recognise that there must now of necessity be areas of overlap between the Fund and Bank owing to the nature of their operations, I want to caution that cross-conditionality should be avoided at all cost.

Indeed, these two institutions; the World Bank and the International Monetary Fund must not appear to be moving in the direction of making their resources less accessible to member countries, but should instead make resources more readily available to those of us most in need of them.

Not only must additional resources be made available to the developing world in order to achieve economic growth and stability, but there is an urgent need for review of the Fund's conditionality provisions under its standby and External Fund Facilities. In addition, consideration should be given to the removal of the quota-based access limits, and increasing conditionality associated with borrowing under the Compensatory Financing Facility. To link borrowings under the Compensatory Financing Facility (CFF) to conditionality guidelines, is to undermine the very purpose for which this facility was established.

The need to augment the resources of the Fund and the Bank, through increased quotas on the one hand, as well as an increase in the capital base on the other, is evident if we are to reverse the adverse trends in resource transfers that have now become characteristic of the global economy, adversely affecting developing countries.

Of even greater importance to low income countries is the replenishment of IDA 8 at the original level, in order to provide the much needed financial assistance. We in the OECS are conscious of the importance to us of access to the Bank's soft loans window, and know that loss of this access will impact adversely on our development prospects when we are no longer eligible for this type of funding from 1990. To compound the problem, we could very well also at this time find ourselves in the position where we may not be considered sufficiently credit-worthy to borrow from the Bank! This in my view would be a serious abdication of one of the key responsibilities of that institution.

I note with some satisfaction the recent establishment of the Structural Adjustment Facility of the Fund, although qualifying members can expect to receive a mere 47% of their quotas over a three year period. The tendency to link the use of SAF Funds with the normal facilities of the Fund and the Bank should not cause preconditions to be imposed on the use of these resources.

While increased resources of both the Fund and Bank will be heralded by the developing world as a move in the right direction, I want to caution that every effort should be made on the part of both these institutions to reduce the lead time between actual submission of proposal and date of first disbursement. As we are all aware, these significant time lags can prove to be very costly, given the continuing escalation of input costs.

Fellow Ministers, let me reiterate: like every other country here, we in the smaller states are striving for economic growth and stability, but we are cognizant that for some time to come, the provision of special financial aid to bring about adjustment of economic growth must be continued and enlarged.

Mr. Chairman, the Commonwealth Finance Ministers meeting should not be just a forum of articulate grumbling about the sins of the world; it has to be a place where a third of the world's countries determine their collective will, and a way forward.

There are two issues, among others, upon which we would like to see this conference resolve its position, and which we should collectively agree to pursue with the Bank and the Fund.

1. Ensure restraint on cross-conditionality: we cannot stop it, but we should restrain it.

2. Ensure that World Bank and IDA resources are expanded by the countries capable of contributing, viz; Germany and Japan. Those who have the greatest control over the policies of the Bank, and to whom the word 'conditionality' is very familiar, should not be alarmed when other lenders seek better conditions for their own loans. We should not leave it up to Japan and the United States to settle this. Developing countries must perceive what is best for them, and anything that is good for increasing IDA resources

such as having the threshold of veto lowered should be supported by us.

References are constantly being made to the need to direct resources from arms expenditure to economic and social development. Indeed, it is rather ironic today that the countries now capable of expanding IDA resources (Germany and Japan) are the ones constitutionally debarred from certain military expenditure.

Mr. Chairman, I am delighted when I hear delegates among us like Sir Julius Chan of Papua, New Guinea refer to the need to put our house in order. I speak with some authority on the subject, because we in St. Vincent and the Grenadines have had the courage to do this in two short years, and while we have not entirely covered the distance in restructuring our economy to withstand storms and international economic forces, we have converted the deficit we inherited into a moderate surplus, with our balance of trade improving, and inflation less than 2%. But if those of us who ARE putting our house in order experience delays in disbursement in one form or another, and are not assisted in moving forward, I wonder what signals are sent to the resolute and the delinquent.

In conclusion, I wish to congratulate St. Lucia for the excellent arrangements made for this conference. We are delighted to have so many Commonwealth friends visit us in this region, so that they can see for themselves how efficiently we are using our slender resources.

Part III

FOREIGN POLICY

FORTIETH ANNIVERSARY ADDRESS TO THE UNITED NATIONS

New York

October 14th, 1985

FORTIETH ANNIVERSARY ADDRESS
TO THE UNITED NATIONS

Mr. President, I wish to congratulate you on your election to the presidency of this historic 40th session of the United Nations General Assembly. As a diplomat experienced in international affairs you are well qualified to guide us through this all important session in the life of the organisation.

My delegation wishes to take this opportunity also to express our gratitude to your predecessor, Ambassador Paul Lukasa, for the skilful and efficient manner in which he presided over the 39th session of the assembly.

I wish too, to offer my compliments to you Mr. Secretary General for the able manner in which you are exercising your responsibilities particularly in the areas of political tension in widely scattered parts of the world. We note with appreciation the report which you have presented to this general assembly and you can be assured, Your Excellency, of the support of the government and people of Saint Vincent and the Grenadines in your tireless task and in your quest for peace, the settlements of disputes, and development for all peoples.

We wish to take this opportunity to express our government's sympathy with the people of Mexico, suffering under the impact of the recent earthquakes. We in the Caribbean know the nature of tragedy caused by volcanic eruptions and hurricanes and trust that the international community will respond positively to the rehabilitation process in Mexico.

For the last 40 years the government and people of the United States, and particularly the city of New York, has hosted this organisation and its delegations. I wish therefore to express my gratitude to New York in particular, and the United States in general for their hospitality to the rest of the world for the last four decades.

Perhaps no other city in the world could have survived the impact of all our varied cultural influences.

Mr. President, forty years after the United Nations came into being the purpose and principles of the organisation laid down at the outset remain as valid today as they were in 1945. The charter has stood the test of time, and the government of Saint Vincent and the Grenadines supports its maintenance in its present form. Whatever the shortcomings in its implementation, or the limitations of the

United Nations institutions, they do not derive from the charter. We would therefore rededicate ourselves to the principles so ably set forth by the Founding Fathers for this body that has served us so well.

Mr. President, St. Vincent and the Grenadines in 1979, in a year of a dislocating volcanic eruption, became the 154th member of this organisation. I would hate to imagine what independence would have meant for a small country like ours with approximately 100,000 people if an organisation like the United Nations did not exist. Small and dependent countries shed by the metropolitan powers would really be drifting aimlessly if an organisation like the United Nations were not there to create a focal point of belonging. Indeed it will not be an exaggeration to congratulate the United Nations for providing a framework for the sovereign existence of small nations.

Perhaps one criticism of the charter that will be voiced on this anniversary, either within these walls or outside, is the right of small countries to the same status of one vote as is the case for larger and more powerful countries. Let me say, however irksome this may have proven over the years, I do not believe it has on balance been the cause of the major problems in the functioning of the United Nations system.

Mr. President, I wish to turn my attention now to those countries denied membership of the United Nations. I trust that when the time comes to celebrate the fiftieth anniversary, there will be no people in the world unrepresented here. The United Nations then will have achieved genuine universality.

Representatives of 149 countries a few days ago attended meetings of the World Bank and International Monetary Fund in the South Korean captital of Seoul. It is ridiculous that the dynamic people of the Republic of Korea are not represented here. We support their right of accession and would hope that the impediments to their membership could be resolved. Recent progress in the Red Cross talks, and also the economic talks between the two Koreas of different ideologies are paving the way for meaningful cooperation. This cooperation must be encouraged, and it is here in the United Nations that dialogue can be given a tangible form of encouragement. Therefore, it is desirable that the members of the United Nations help create a better political environment for a peaceful solution of the Korean question by encouraging both Koreas to continue the dialogue. The admittance of both Koreas as members of the United Nations may assist in reducing tensions and creating peace in the Korean Peninsula.

Another country denied access to full membership is the Territory of Namibia. St. Vincent and the Grenadines believes that the basis of any definitive solution to the Namibian problem are contained in Security Council Resolution 435 and urges the International Body to seek its early implementation.

Over the past forty years, there has been no more intractable problem than the conflict in the Middle East. No part of the world has escaped the impact of the controversy between Israel and the Palestinians. Small countries have absolutely no control in the resolution of such a conflict, but the conflict has had and continues to have an influence from time to time on economic conditions which adversely affect us and since we in St. Vincent and the Grenadines are not immune, we must place our position on record. We recognise the right of Israel to exist, and also support the right of the Palestinians to a homeland. We pray that the stalemate in the Middle East created by the denial of a homeland to the Palestinians will not continue to drag on interminably.

In the interest of world peace and security we look forward to a peaceful resolution to the dispute within the framework of the United Nations Charter and one which would satisfy the just aspirations of all the peoples of the region.

Mr. President, it is praiseworthy that during the forty years of its existence the United Nations has steadfastly endeavoured to implement the charter objectives of promoting respect for and the observance of human rights and fundamental freedoms for all. The numerous international conventions and declarations concluded under its auspices give expression to the moral conscience of mankind and represent humanitarian standards for all members of the international community. However, my delegation is aware that in spite of the manifold efforts of the United Nations in this field, serious violations of human rights are still being committed against individuals and groups in several areas of the world. In our country, my government has provided opportunity for expression which not long ago was denied us, and we will continue to promote respect for all of our citizens without regard to race, colour, sex or religion.

Of all the crises in the world today, the growing conflict between the minority regime and the liberation movement in South Africa is of most direct and urgent concern to the United Nations. We in the Caribbean who have experienced the conditions of colonialism and whose populations are characterised by much the same racial blending bewteen Africa, Europe and India are at a loss to understand the lack of faith in racial harmony that may evolve in due process of time. The government and people of St. Vincent and the Grenadines condemn the evil policy of apartheid which is a crime against humanity and which is contrary to all the principles of the charter. We pledge ourselves to do all we can, in accordance with the letter and spirit of the charter, to assist in the elimination of apartheid in South Africa.

We consider what is particularly important in this regard, in terms of securing results in facing the mighty machine of government in South Africa, is that the international community continues to give a clear and unambiguous signal that the status quo has absolutely no historical chance of being sustained. Change is the first basic law of the universe, and secondly, nature abhors a vacuum. The vacuum prescribed for the majority has had its walls shattered. What is needed now is serious dialogue among the leadership of the races in South Africa to create a constitutional framework for the evolution of harmony among all races in South Africa based on the principle of one man, one vote.

Mr. President, I now turn to some of the problems of our region. In reference to peace and security in our hemisphere the government of St. Vincent and the Grenadines wishes to place on record our support for the Contadora Process. We feel that those of us who are committed to peaceful reform are the best hope for the evolution of Democracy within the region and our judgement should be trusted accordingly.

Mr. President, there are two developmental issues which are of utmost importance and which the United Nations will need to continue to address. They are the burdens of the debtor nations, and the high rate of populations increase in poor countries.

Global economic recovery continues to be tentative but is being further stymied by increased protectionism in world trade, which effectively reduces the capacity of developing countries to service their debt and sustain economic growth, since a larger portion of revenue is being utilized for debt servicing.

Limited advances have been made in our region only through stringent structural adjustment policies with severe human cost particularly for the poorest sections of our society.

Where limited improvements have been effected these have been outstripped by population increases. Our region's labour force has expanded beyond the level that can be sustained by our economic activity and thus rising unemployment continues to challenge our economic well-being.

This brings me to my second concern, that is, population planning. I wish to place on record our support for the United Nations Fund for population activities. In this regard, I wish to state, however, that each country should be free to determine its own strategy for population activities. There should be no attempt to impose moral standards on others. I will go further and state that it is immoral to impose the morality of the rich on poor countries whose increase in economic activity is nullified by excessive population growth.

Mr. President, Your Excellencies, Distinguished Delegates, I wish to express my humble opinion on the spectacle of vast expenditure on arms as seen by us as representatives of the poor. I am not one to invite mankind to cease extending the boundaries of our knowledge. Scientific research continues to improve the condition of mankind, but to think that there will be a new way that a defense initiative will not be undermined once more by espionage preying on human weakness is to ignore the lessons of the last forty years.

What is the point of spending billions on secretive defense which experience has told us espionage will sooner or later render useless! Far better I think to address the problems of poverty and development and strengthen the economies of those who want to be stronger partners in a free world. It will never be too late to pursue that other goal shared by the rich and poor alike, even though in varying degrees, to improve the quality of life. Let us never tire of urging this option in the councils that matter as we approach the close of our century.

Mr. President, I wish to congratulate the Secretary General and the Preparatory Committee for the work they have put into organising this fortieth anniversary. Anniversaries are suitable occasions to reflect on the past and plan for the future. My delegation rededicates itself to supporting the United Nations Charter and its institutions. An organisation that continues to accommodate the tense rivalries among us deserves our support. Thank you, Mr. President.

COMMONWEALTH ADDRESS

Address at the Opening Ceremony of the
Commonwealth Heads of Government Meeting
Vancouver

October 14th, 1987

COMMONWEALTH ADDRESS 1987

It is for me a distinct pleasure to return to Vancouver at this Commonwealth Heads of Government Conference.

When it was decided that Canada was going to be our host country I was very happy indeed, but when I learned that Vancouver was to be our host city, I was absolutely overjoyed.

I left this city and the University of British Columbia some thirty years ago, and I certainly never dreamed then that I would one day return as Prime Minister of St. Vincent and the Grenadines to this magnificent city and this beautiful province which nurtured me so kindly in the wandering days of my youth.

The road back to Vancouver has not been through any elegant garden of roses. Such is not the way, for any of us gathered here on this rostrum, in becoming a Head of Government, on either a small island or a large continent.

Mr. Chairman, I hope you will forgive a bit of speculation on my part. It could well be that my days as a student in Vancouver in the mid-fifties preceded the first visit of the young Brian Mulroney to this city, so I shall take the liberty, Mr. Prime Minister, to welcome you to my old hometown.

I wish on behalf of my Caribbean colleagues—the President of Guyana and the Prime Ministers of Antigua and Barbuda, Barbados, Belize, Dominica, Grenada, Jamaica, St. Kitts and Nevis, St. Lucia, and Trinidad and Tobago— to thank you, Prime Minister Mulroney, and the Government and people of Canada, for hosting this Commonwealth Conference. We are indeed overwhelmed by your traditional Canadian hospitality.

We would certainly wish to congratulate the Governments of Canada and of the Province of British Columbia, as well as Secretary General Ramphal and his staff, for the very excellent arrangements you all have made for this Conference.

My presence here, Mr. Chairman, is living testimony to the heritage and traditions we share in this English speaking Commonwealth. Many, too, are the other Kings, Presidents, Prime Ministers, Ministers and delegates among us here today who still fondly cherish the memories of their youth in Canada and in other metropolitan countries. But sadly, we who obtained much of our higher education away from home are a vanishing breed, and even though we consider it necessary and proper to develop our own indigenous institutions, the Commonwealth as a whole is much poorer for the diminution of opportunity for international student exchange. The exorbitant charges on foreign students abroad today is a recipe for nationalistic chauvinism. I would hope that as the economies in industrial countries strengthen, the way will be seen to restore some quota of educational opportunity for young people at reasonable cost in foreign universities. This Conference will need no reminding that some of the severe problems our world faces, for example, the debt crisis and its negative impact on economic growth, and the problems of over-population, have their genesis in the failings of the human resource.

We will be addressing in this Conference the problems of global communications, and proposals for a programme that will create educational opportunities by satellite to the remotest villages in the world. This is commendable, and we should all give it every support, for hopefully it will bring some positive training to counterbalance much that is irrelevant to us on the satellite screens. But there is no substitute for the studying and living experience of a young person away from home, learning, for instance, how to cope with winter, and witnessing the values and work ethic that make the industrial world a success. There will be no substitute for the coffee shop indulgence in mid-winter, and the youthful fraternising that leads later to international camaraderie in the professions, in business, or in the conference halls. While we, in the Commonwealth of free nations, cut short the mutual historical advantages and cultural linkages we once shared, others, with a more sinister agenda, are rushing in to fill the void.

Those of us who have found our way beyond the jungle of useless concepts and slogans that have only served to retard the progress of our civilization owe it to the less fortunate to wet them on the tested path that we know will provide self-sustaining growth and the quality of life that guarantees a more beautiful world. If this perception is clear, let us not evade the responsibility to train and lead young people in the direction we think is best for them, and the kind of world we want to continue to create.

At these conferences, the Commonwealth expresses its views on the burning economic and political issues of the day. It is usual to pay some special attention to the problems of the micro-states. On this occasion, the delegations of the East Caribbean will hope to focus some attention and seek the support of the Commonwealth in our quest for political unity in our region. Those of us who refuse to allow our imagination to be trapped in the bondage of our history have begun a process of consultation with the people which, if successful, will represent the first occasion since the establishment of the United Nations, that independent countries would have merged their sovereignty. The Commonwealth has been at great pains to try to create a meaningful role for small states in the international community. Indeed, the Commonwealth has been very indulgent of and sympathetic to the inherent problems of smallness in the international arena. We appreciate your magnanimity and your forbearance, but some of us in the small States have come to recognise that there is only one inevitable solution to our problems, and that is to unite our several small countries into a single nation. This language must certainly touch a responsive chord in North America, for the strength of your vast countries of Canada and the United States derives from the historic decisions of the great founding fathers of your nations. The same arguments, with which the founding fathers in North America battled, are the identical ones with which we have to take issue in our mini-states several centuries later. The only irony is that the current advocates of the status quo genuinely believe that they have originality on their side!

We have come to these conclusions from our own experience in asserting our independence internationally and in reference to the internal inadequacies at the national level. No one has sought to impose this thinking upon us: it has emerged, of necessity, out of our experience and out of our anxiety to provide the quality of life that our corner of the world should produce. Mr. Chairman, no one can prepare us for the problems of the twenty-first century. We can be assisted in our preparations and adjustments, but it is up to us to perceive the realities ourselves as we recognise the fragility of our individual economies, our slender resource base, and our vulnerability to the forces of nature.

With Canada and the United States contemplating the creation of a single market, and with the quickened pace of economic integration in Europe, it becomes even more incumbent on small islands like ours to learn from these examples.

I would hope that this conference will give its blessing to our aspirations to political unification in the East Caribbean. I know that if we succeed, we will be sending very important signals even to those in the rest of the world who have greater resources than ourselves.

Our other problems in the Caribbean are the familiar and general international concerns such as the debt crisis, protectionism, and the low prices for certain commodities. It is our hope that the new incentives to supplement resources of the International Monetary Fund and the restructuring of the Caribbean Basin Initiative and the United States Congress will provide us with the tools of our economic recovery commensurable with the progress in the rest of the world.

In Nassau, we worked very hard to produce a consensus on Southern Africa. We in the Caribbean who historically have experienced various degrees of exploitation, and whose populations are characterised by much the same racial origins from Africa, Europe and Asia as there are in South Africa, are at a loss to understand why there is so little faith in the racial harmony that could evolve in due process of time if all of the people in Southern Africa were treated equally under the law. The people of the Caribbean remain uncompromisingly opposed to apartheid.

It is our hope that this conference will maintain the Nassau momentum for a resolution of the problems in South Africa, Namibia, and the front line States in a manner that sustains the values for which this Commonwealth stands, and that will bring new hope to the deprived peoples of Southern Africa.

Mr. Chairman, I cannot close without taking this opportunity to thank the taxpayers of Canada, who through succeeding Governments have generously assisted in our development in the Caribbean. St. Vincent and the Grenadines and the rest of the Caribbean enjoy working closely with Canada in the international community. I wish also to thank Canada for being host to so many Caribbean people.

Meetings of the Commonwealth Heads of Government will always produce several statements, but none of these really reveal the fraternity which these meetings engender, a fraternity which keeps these very different regions of the world united in spirit, and graciously presided over by our Queen.

UNITED NATIONS ON DISARMAMENT

*Address to the Third Session of the United
Nations General Assembly Devoted to Disarmament
New York*

June 13th, 1988

UNITED NATIONS ON DISARMAMENT

Mr. President, on behalf of the Government and People of St. Vincent and the Grenadines, permit me to add my voice to all the delegations which have preceeded me in congratulating you upon your election to the Presidency of this Special Session of the United Nations General Assembly Devoted to Disarmament. We are confident that with your vast experience and diplomatic skills you will guide this Session to a successful conclusion.

May I also convey our appreciation to the Secretary General, Mr. Javier Perez De Cuellar, for the role which he continues to play in the development of the Organisation, and in particular, for his commitment to international peace, co-operation and development.

Mr. President, the final document unanimously adopted at the First Special Session on disarmament is still the most authoritative statement that has been made on disarmament. It proposed a wide range of measures intended to enhance the security of nations at progressively lower levels of armaments, and stressed the central role and primary responsibility of the United Nations in the field of disarmament.

This Third Special Session provides a collective opportunity for reviewing the progress made over the past ten years. It is an opportunity also for assessing the adequacy and effectiveness of the disarmament machinery, and drawing up a programme of action for the remaining years of the present century.

This session, unlike the Second Special Session in 1982, takes place against a background of improved relations between the Superpowers and some decrease in the level of international tension. Positive development in the international situation are witnessed by the recently concluded INF Treaty between the USSR and the USA, the Geneva Agreement on Afghanistan with the withdrawal of all foreign troops from that country, the Stockholm Conference on Confidence—and Security—Building Measures and Disarmament in Europe, renewed activity on the part of NATO and the Warsaw Treaty Organisation aimed at reducing the levels of their conventional forces.

Mr. President, the task which the international community set itself in the programme of action in the Final Document of the First Special Session on Disarmament is far from being achieved. The treaty between the USA and the USSR on the elimination of their intermediate range and shorter range missiles is an important psychological breakthrough. It is the first time in their present cycle of negotiations that the Superpowers have been able to agree to eliminate a whole category of weapons, thus initiating action in the area of true disarmament as distinct from arms limitation.

Mr. President, this session now derives added significance as it comes in the wake of the recent historic meeting in Moscow between General Secretary Gorbachev and President Reagan.

I am authorised by the countries of the East Caribbean to congratulate President Reagan and General Secretary Gorbachev on their historic achievement. We see significance not only in the Treaty banning the deployment of intermediate and short range missiles but in the signals of the mood of change in Superpower confrontation which every country in the United Nations System should do all in their power to encourage.

We the small countries of the world recognise that the mood of conflict generated during the Cold War contributed in large measure to the pace of decolonisation over the last forty years and created opportunities for our Independence.

We are however, prepared to look positively on the easing of tensions of the Superpowers which we recognise to constitute the new basis of hope for the improvement of the quality of life for those who love this beautiful world that God has given us and those whom we want to inherit it.

It is our wish that the process of arms reduction by the Superpowers will gain momentum and stabilise at a level that will ensure their security and ours.

We would want to see a comparable easing of tension in regional conflicts, particularly in the Middle East and Central America.

Mr. President, while it is fashionable to blame the arms race on the Superpowers and the industrial powers, attention must also be focused on those other countries which devote inordinate amounts of their budgets to arms purchases. There are very few countries in the world that could not benefit from directing expenditure from arms toward expanding their health and anti-poverty programmes.

Mr. President, never since the invention of the nuclear weapon and the arms race it sponsored, has there been a more opportune time for the reversal of the arms race than now, and we must seek to find ways to build on the success of the Moscow Summit. We must all encourage that process if we are interested in peace and improvement in the quality of life in the world.

The thinking of General Secretary Gorbachev has produced a unique opportunity for political restructuring in the rest of the world. We will not be naive in our assessment of progress, and we will rely on those with the capacity to execute the responsibility for verification of arms reduction. As this proceeds, we would urge that everything be done to ensure that the momentum of reduction be sustained, and similarly, this ought to be supported by universal progress in the reduction of conventional weapons, and the easing of regional conflicts. Our "moral persuasion" must extend to the regional conflicts also.

In the long march of history from the invention of gunpowder up to the ultimate in the creation of nuclear weapons millions have died in the struggle for dominance by various peoples and various dogmas.

The Moscow Summit may yet be the greatest turning point in this history. The question we must ask is: How many more millions must die in the pursuit of mistaken policies that eventually have to be reversed!

"*Perestroika*" has created a unique opportunity in the presistent pattern of conflicts, and this, coupled with the response it has engendered in the United States, gives us cause to celebrate, and it is an opportunity to celebrate that we must not miss. Indeed, it has been too dangerous a road between TNT and the INF Treaty not to deserve a celebration of its conclusion.

Nuclear arms threatened life on this planet. We support the view that savings from disarmament should be channelled into development. There are many developement demands, and in my view, funds saved would be most efficiently used if redirected into a single project. I propose the urgent task of Reafforestation in Africa, halting the march of the desert as the highest priority. This is the way we propose to celebrate. No human thought produced results that threatened our environment so terribly, and if this threat recedes, we can do nothing greater than apply these scarce resources for the enhancement of our environment.

Mr. President, this is not a project in which we the people of the Caribbean will benefit directly, but we are made sensitive to this great need by the increasing frequency of

Sahara haze clouding our visibility in the Caribbean. But, above all, we will be only too happy to help focus attention to the continent in desperate need of environmental therapy, and one that claims our ancestral roots. With this problem addressed on a global scale, with resources created by disarmament, there will be other sources freed up to meet our own needs for development finance.

But to access these funds on this project, or any other that may be agreed upon apart from my priority, there should be conditionality. The guideline should impose a simple rule of accessing funds, namely; that recepient countries of disarmament funds should themselves be reducing their military expenditure. It certainly will not be logical to be calling on the superpowers and the industrial nations to reduce conventional arms while we in the Third World reconstitute ourselves into new markets for conventional weapons.

Creating a special fund for use of disarmament savings will in itself keep the need to accelerate the creation and release of those funds in constant focus.

Mr. President, in St. Vincent and the Grenadines, and the Caribbean for which I speak, our declared policy is to concentrate on economic development as the surest way to ease the social tensions. We do not perceive our insecurity as curable by military options.

The world has been watching with fascination in the last few days the monumental progress made at the Moscow Summit. Coming on the heels of Moscow, this disarmament session must create a role for itself beyond being described as a side show. We will do so only by creating a new role for the United Nations in Disarmament, even in the fashion I suggest or any other that may arise, and in so doing fortify the essential and fundamental purpose of this august body. Even, therefore, as we move forward in new directions, we consolidate the foundations long established in the architecture of the United Nations Charter.

ZAMBIA: COURAGE, SACRIFICE AND CHALLENGES

Address at Quinquennial Conference of the
United National Indepence Party of Zambia
Mulungushi, Zambia

August 19th, 1988

ZAMBIA: COURAGE, SACRIFICE AND CHALLENGES

Your Excellency Dr. Kenneth Kaunda, President of the Republic of Zambia, Mr. Chairman, Mr. Prime Minister, Chief Justice, Fellow Heads of State and Heads of Government, Distinguished Members of the Central Committee of the United National Independence Party of Zambia, Honourable Ministers, Ambassadors and High Commissioners, Brothers and Sisters of Zambia. I am deeply honoured to be in your presence today.

The delegation of St. Vincent and the Grenadines includes; my Attorney General and Chairman of our New Democratic Party, the Honourable Parnel Campbell, and our Ambassador to the United Nations, His Excellency Mr. Jonathan Peters.

We are all extremely delighted to be with you on this momentous occasion, an historic congress that meets to chart the future of Zambia in her crucial role in the history of Southern Africa: historic too, at this crucial time in the closing decade of the twentieth century.

Brothers and Sisters, to be born in the Caribbean, by virtue of being born in that part of the world, means that from one's very conception, Africa means a great deal to the individual. Africa, by and large, constitutes our genetic motherland. To visit Africa therefore, becomes an ambition of every inquiring mind in the Caribbean, an ambition which unfortunately is hardly affordable by the majority of Caribbean sons and daughters. For us, this visit to Africa is the fulfilment of a dream. But coming to Zambia is a very special privilege. The people of the Caribbean recognise Zambia as a leading frontline state, not only in the struggle for the liberation of Southern Africa, but also in the struggle against colonialism everywhere.

To come to Zambia as Prime Minister of a Caribbean country and President of my party, and to address the United National Independence Party of Zambia will, for me, remain one of the most cherished moments of my life. It therefore gives me a sense of personal fulfilment to bring to you, the People of the Republic of Zambia, fraternal greetings and pledges of solidarity from the People of St. Vincent and the Grenadines, from the Central Committee and the Brothers and Sisters of my New Democratic Party, and messages of continuing support from the people of the Caribbean as a whole.

When in October last year in Vancouver, a city in which I had been educated, and where I addressed the Peoples of the Commonwealth at the opening of the Commonwealth Heads of Government on behalf of the Caribbean, your distinguished President invited me to address this Congress, I prayed that Heaven would sustain me until I set foot on your soil.

This is my first visit to Africa, and it is a delight for me to begin my African experience in Zambia. I am only sorry that I do not have my family here with me on this occasion. Many of my Ministers, as well as Ambassadors Peters, have attended various conferences in Africa, but for my Attorney General and myself, this is our first mission and I can assure you, it will not be our last.

I want to assure you that hardly a day goes by that Southern Africa is not news in the Caribbean. We still have colonies in the Caribbean, but that colonialism is a result of insularity, microstatus and scale, and all of these colonies have democratically elected governments with the attendant freedoms. So when I say the news in the Caribbean concerns itself with Southern Africa, I mean that the people of the Caribbean, one and all, concern themselves with affairs in this part of the world, and Caribbean consciousness embraces a special sensitivity to the troubles of Africa.

I have met your distinguished President Dr. Kenneth Kaunda at the Nassau and Vancouver summits. What I would like you and this party in Zambia to know, and emphasize what you ought to be aware of, is that in Kenneth Kaunda you have a leader, brilliant as any in this world; a man who, when he speaks, commands the attention of the international community. It is not merely his longevity in office that commands respect. It is the principles for which he and Zambia have stood over the decades. It is what he says, the way he says it, and the manifest substance of the man which constitutes authority. We, who have the privilege to be leaders, know that we cannot rely on any speech we have given in the past to carry us through any new presentation; every speech must stand on its own merit and from what I experienced in Vancouver, the best speeches of Kenneth Kaunda may not be heard by the world at large. In the secret halls of the Vancouver conference, when the press had been firmly excluded, it was there, only in the presence of his peers, that Kenneth Kaunda aroused the conscience of the Commonwealth, and brought tears to the eyes of many, in a way that none of us who were honoured to be present on that occasion will ever forget. When the time comes, as it should, as it must, that South Africa is liberated, the Azanians will have failed Africa if they do not establish monuments in recognition of the heroes in their struggle for their liberation, and I say they will have failed themselves and disappointed the world if special recognition is not given to Kenneth Kaunda.

Now, distinguished delegates, brothers and sisters, in his invitation to me, your President indicated that you will be evaluating your country's policies and strategies as required by the progressive peoples of the world for the development of Zambia.

1988 constitutes a very significant turning point in the history of international conflict, and in its train, regional conflict. We are into the era of *"Perestroika"* and *"Glasnost"*, a phrase that included the significant Reagan Presidency, when mountains of arms are to be dispensed with, and more significantly, the accompanying myths are being destroyed. The framework of Rapproachement creates new opportunities for the resolution of regional conflicts, and at the same time, if not creatively applied, can produce new hazards. With the sting being taken out of the fear of the advance of international communism, with the restructuring of policy in the Soviet Union, and also the fundamental changes taking place in the People's Republic of China, the consideration which sponsored assistance to Third World countries, particularly to those which were in conflict with their neighbours, may well be reassessed. International attention in the aftermath of the Second World War, we may recall, created opportunities for our independence. It created opportunities in the struggle for freedom in Africa. Now, as the Americans will say, there is a new ball game in town. We in the Third World must continue to make the correct analysis and fashion our strategies accordingly.

But while one must be cautious, even as we can articulate the fear of being abandoned to our regional conflicts, if spheres of influence are no longer the catchword in international rivalry, we must recognise the events in the wake of *"Perestroika"*: the peace process in Vietnam and Cambodia, Iran and Iraq, and new opportunities in Angola and Namibia.

We are now into a critical phase, a critical time. It calls for clear thinking, rational appraisal, quick decisions. There is a momentum now for peace that has not existed since the advent of the Cold War. And before new trends and tensions create new conflicts, now is the time to press home the opportunity, as we see it, for Independence for Namibia, and getting one step closer to inevitable freedom in South Africa.

Now as the strategic climate of the international struggle changes, more emphasis will be placed on economic development and this is another race we cannot afford to lose. At the Third Special Session at the United Nations in June, I put forward an idea to create a Special United Nations Fund for savings that should emanate from disarmament. I went further and suggested that a non-controversial project be earmarked as the first to use these funds, namely, the re-afforestation of Africa. I am pleased to be in a position to tell you that the idea that these funds be given priority use in Africa, was widely accepted in the Caribbean.

I think it is important that we focus some international attention on disarmament savings. We can expect the argument that disarmament is controversial in many countries, and that in order to maintain the momentum of disarmament, industrial countries will have to spend the savings at home to convince their own taxpayers of the benefits of disarmament. We can expect as well that the relative expenditures in various countries will be on the table; some countries will argue that their percentage expenditure on arms is nationally low and that they will wait on others to reduce theirs first. But in my view, the creation of a fund is essential if there is going to be a focal thrust for disarmament.

I beg your indulgence to present to the International Community, a second proposal. If the Industrial Countries and Nuclear Powers fail to create a disarmament fund, then we should press along a second front. The direction I propose is that a challenge be carried to the Industrial Nations that in the light of reduction of expenditure on arms they meet the international aid target of 0.7% of GDP. Surely, with super power tensions now being reduced, and global security now coming within reach, the way forward is to build the economies of the world where real growth would be most advantageous to all concerned.

Our world makes progress with the evolution of ideas, and we must move with these new ideas. Collectively in the Third World we should see how we can respond creatively to the new opportunities made possible by new ideas.

Now is the time for us to mount a revitalised campaign on that 0.7% contribution to aid. We must do so in every forum, in every international meeting, until we bring this theme back into the limelight. It is an international commitment brushed aside in the plethora of statistics on the world debt situation. It deserves its own constant analysis and publicity.

We the beneficiaries of that aid know only too well and in real terms that that figure, when its technical assistance and procurement procedures are exercised, is considerably less in the poor recipient countries.

PART II

In preparation for coming to this convention, I have been looking at your progress and challenges in Zambia, as your published figures indicate. I am therefore basically familiar with the kind of situation I see your economy facing and the pressures your people have to endure. The world should not forget that Zambia continues to pay a high price for the resolute and principled stand it has taken over the years in the pursuit of human dignity in Africa and elsewhere. Nor must it be forgotten that freedom carries a high price. I would hope, Mr. President, that the Members of your Party, and the people of your country, would understand that the sacrifices they have made and are continuing to make are not in vain. People of Zambia, I salute you!

Let me, with your indulgence, say something about my own country and its present finances. Our Party took over the reins of government in 1984, and found a situation of bankruptcy. On our small island scale, there was massive but manageable debt, a deficit on current account, and a general malaise in the community. Fortunately for me, when my Party won in 1984, I had had before the eighteen years of Parliamentary experience, including the period as Premier during the energy crisis in 1973—1974, and I was clear on the direction we wanted to pursue.

We set about restructuring our economy and government finances on our own. We did not wait on the International Monetary Fund and any Fund programme. We had to take painful political decisions. We took them early. Some of these decisions were quite unpopular and even somewhat stalwart members of the Party expressed their fears for the possible political consequences, but my Cabinet colleagues and I stood firm. We listened to the people. We gave them every opportunity, even on radio, to ventilate their grievances. But today, with the positive economic results brought about by some of these initially unpopular policies, it is now being recognised that very often a particular medicine, though unpleasant to the taste, may be the only cure for a particular ailment.

Today we in St. Vincent and the Grenadines are the beneficiaries of that restructuring. We can service our debt. Our inflation is below three percent. We have had a surplus on current account for the last years, and now we project a balanced budget as we face elections. We have gone through our structural adjustment. There are many opinions on the price of economic restructuring the world over, but the view to which I subscribe is that there is one thing worse than structural adjustment, and that is, no structural adjustment. The longer the decisions are left, the worse is the medicine to be applied: and then the body politic hardly has the energy to withstand the shock.

I do hope that as the tensions in Namibia and Angola and this region ease, you can see the way to move in directions that will maximise the development of your abundant resources. The people of many Third World countries get caught up in the glamour of so called modernisation and rush to the cities to be wage earners, rather than farmers, only to find that their greatest household bill is for food. Departing from the wisdom of their forefathers, they choose to become the employees of other people in the cities rather than preserving their dignity by being their own bosses on their own farms.

In working out a development strategy, it is useful that we look around us to see what has produced success elsewhere. Those of us who travel and who lead opinion at home, should not fail to tell our people what it is like flying over Europe and North America, watching the abundant fields of well-tended agriculture. The strength of the industrial countries is not only their efficiency in industrial production or their advanced technology, it is in their agriculture. By feeding themselves, they have that balance of payments generated by all kinds of exports of surpluses. We in the Third World, therefore must go back to the land and feed ourselves as a fundamental tenet and concept of development. The strategies that bring this about must be constantly re-evaluated.

There are success stories around us in the Third World. That of food production is the success story of India. Who would have thought that India's millions could feed themselves? They have done so. In turn we hear more now of India's export potential in many fields.

Mr. Chairman, Distinguished Heads of State, permit me to say a few words outside my originally prepared text to reinforce the concerns expressed yesterday by President Kaunda about bush fires and the drying up of rivers and to comment on what I have witnessed since being in Zambia. President Museveni of Uganda yesterday also spoke of Africa's need for science, technology and management.

I am myself, apart from being a political leader, an agricultural scientist. Let me in all humility offer a word of advice. On my State visit you kindly took us as far north as the Copper Belt and south to Livingstone. I was absolutely appalled at the hundreds of bush fires we saw everywhere, and vast areas burnt to cinder. When you burn the grass, you destroy the humus, the organic matter, the trees. The grass returns, not the trees. Eventually the grass too will not return. You destroy the fertility of your land, you destroy the humidity, you destroy your future. If you love Zambia, do not burn her. This is my advice to your people, Mr. President, in all humility.

To continue Mr. President, as you look about for new strategies in development, let me draw to your attention our experience in tourism: that it is the fastest growing foreign exchange earner among the economic sectors. You here in Zambia may well be thinking of doing a lot more in this field, but let me caution you that if you do, you ought to determine early and precisely what model of tourism you will pursue.

The mass market can bring you early wide publicity, but not enduring growth. It is best above all to determine your own model, expand your own indigenous architecture and cuisine, while you match the internationally established and required standards of service. You may be interested in pursuing what is called in certain parts of Mexico, "ECO Tourism", the concentration on marketing your environment, your ecology, the inherent qualities of your geography and your historical culture. This model aims at a specialised and durable market, for that group of people who enjoy this world as it is.

There are also success stories in the methodology of the

new Industrial Countries of the Pacific, those who have signalled that the twenty-first century is theirs to dominate. We should try and get those lessons into our societies, so that we too can move forward.

We the people of the Caribbean whose lives are saturated with the television screen cannot feel happy when we see the scenes of war and famine in Ethiopia or other parts of Africa. When Africa suffers, we weep. When Africa bleeds, we mourn. When your economies shrink, we despair. We want to see Africa strong. We want an Africa of which we can be proud.

PART III

The message I gave in Vancouver, and the message that may have helped to bring me here, is the statement I made, that we in the Caribbean, being a blend of Africa, Europe and India, are at a loss to understand why South Africans have no faith in the future of racial harmony. I am, myself, a product of that harmony, a genetic blend of Africa, France and England, a product of centuries of conflict, and I know, and we know in the Caribbean that racial harmony is possible on every front, be it spiritual or hard economic ritual. We would not survive without it, and it quantifies our success.

We in the Caribbean will always stand in solidarity with the oppressed people in Southern Africa. As I said in Vancouver last year, we remain unalterably opposed to Apartheid. We want to see all of you in Southern Africa strong, maximising the use of your abundant resources, and getting the world to know you as a beautiful place, not one with a constant and persistent image of conflict. In this world, we are interdependent, and the interdependence of nations, races, cultures, and economies will intensify and not diminish.

The communication age, this new age of information, will make this interdependence even more inevitable than it has been. To go against this trend of interdependence will be futile. Every hour the pace of development quickens. As it quickens, it behooves us all to evaluate the consequences of our being left further and further behind. Those of us whose responsibility it is to lead must be in the forefront of determination of new strategies and policies. Let us all command the future, not merely be responding to its inevitable directions.

You, the people of Zambia, have a wise and tested old leader. You are lucky. I remember my first glimpse of Kenneth Kaunda. It was not, Mr. President, at the Nassau Summit. I remember as a young man I took part in a rally in the early sixties at Trafalgar Square in London, listening with rapture to your anguished cries for Northern and Southern Rhodesia. We have both come a long way since then.

Today is for me a special day, a special anniversary that I am pleased to spend with you at the UNIP Congress. Today, twenty two years ago was the day of my first election to Parliament.

We are pleased to be with you today in Mulunguishi. We thank you for the excellent arrangements for our reception and comfort. I wish you Mr. President, good health and long life. I wish this convention every success. May I take this opportunity, Mr. President, to invite you and your Prime Minister to St. Vincent and the Grenadines at a time of your convenience, to see the land and islands and people from where we bring greetings today.

We are not graced with the majesty of your Victoria Falls, but the beauty of the varied islands in our country is unmatched throughout the Caribbean.

Above all, though we are small and without economic clout in this mighty universe, we are second to none in the moral fortitude we bring to bear on the problems of Southern Africa, and in that spirit we bring our own undiluted joy to this Convention of the United National Independence Party of the Republic of Zambia.

Long live the leadership of Zambia!

Long live the friendship now established between the people of St. Vincent and the Grenadines and the Republic of Zambia.

GLOSSARY OF ABBREVIATIONS

ACP	African Caribbean and Pacific Countries
AMP	Agricultural Marketing Protocol
BVI	British Virgin Islands
BWIA	British West Indies Airlines
CADEC	Christian Action for Development in the East Caribbean
CARIFTA	Caribbean Free Trade Association
CBI	Caribbean Basin Initative
CDB	Caribbean Development Bank
CDU	Caribbean Democrat Union
CFF	Compensatory Financing Facility
DPP	Director of Public Prosecutions
ECCM	East Caribbean Common Market
ESP	Economic Support Program
GDP	Gross Domestic Product
IBRD	International Bank for Reconstruction and Development
IDA	International Development Association
IDA 8	International Development Association 8th Replenishment
IMF	International Monetary Fund
IUPUI	Indiana University and Purdue University in Indiana
J&LSC	Judical and Legal Services Commission
LIAT	Leeward Islands Air Transport
MDC	More Developed Country
NATO	North Alantic Treaty Organisation
NDP	New Democratic Party
OAS	Organisation of American States
OECS	Organisation of Eastern Caribbean States
ONR	Orgainsation for National Reconstruction
SAF	Special Adjustment Facility
SDR	Special Drawing Rights

Exchange value $1.00 US is equal to $2.64 Eastern Caribbean Dollars.

About the author;

James F. Mitchell, commonly known as "Son", was born in Bequia in 1931. He studied agriculture at the Imperial College of Tropical Agriculture, and specialised in agronomy at the University of British Columbia, Canada.

First elected as a Member of Parliament for the Grenadines in 1966, he has remained the elected representative there ever since. Additionally, he has administered several ministries and he is the Founder and President of the New Democratic Party.

Currently Mr. Mitchell bears the title of The Right Honourable James F. Mitchell, Privy Councillor, and is the Prime Minister of St. Vincent and the Grenadines.

As Prime Minister, he resides in St. Vincent, but maintains a home in Bequia. He has three daughters who are studying in Canada.